W9-AXC-551

Marilyn Manson

Manson

Kurt B. Reighley

ST. MARTIN'S GRIFFIN ≋ NEW YORK

Design by Casey Hampton

Library of Congress Cataloging-in-Publication Data

Reighley, Kurt B.
    Marilyn Manson / Kurt B. Reighley.
        p.   cm.
    ISBN 0–312–18133–7
    1. Marilyn Manson (Musical group)   2. Rock musicians—United States—Biography.   I. Title.
ML421.M387R45   1998
782.42166'092'2—dc21
[B]   97–46172
                                                                        CIP
                                                                        MN

First St. Martin's Griffin Edition: May 1998

10   9   8   7   6   5   4   3   2   1

C⊙NTENTS

ACKNOWLEDGMENTS

MY UNDYING GRATITUDE TO my own unholy trinity—Veronica Kirchoff, Paula O'Keefe, and Scott Mitchell (alias Daisy Berkowitz)—for all their help. Without the interviews they graciously granted, and the wealth of research materials they supplied, this book would be much poorer indeed.

For various contributions, great and small, I lovingly tip my hat to: Michael Azerrad; Joe Banks, Rob Cherry, Jason Pettigrew and Norman Wonderly of *Alternative Press*; Blanche Barton of the Church of Satan; Rusty Benson of the *American Family Association Journal*; Nicole Blackman; Paul Bloch; Randy Bookasta of *RayGun*; Carrie Borzillo and the fine folks at allstarmag.com; David "Dog Boy" Brockman; Jason Cohen; Amanda Conquy of Dahl & Dahl; Donna L. Cross; Glenn Danzig; Melissa Dragich at Epic Records; Morgan Engle; Scott Frampton at *CMJ New Music Monthly*; Yvonne Garrett; Tom Gogola; Fiona Hallowell at HarperCollins; Michael Hukin; Martin Huxley; Melissa Kapustey; Jim Kenefick; Michael Krugman; Neil Lawi at Sony Music; Colin McComb; the office of Dan Matthews at PeTA; Lisa Matson; Moby; Maria Castello at London Features; Christine Muhlke of *Paper*; Chris Nickson; Judy Pope; Dan

Renehan; the staff of *Seconds*; Paul Semel; Perry Serpa at Nasty Little Man; Patrick J. Shriner; Vickie Starr; Eric Vetter at Orbit Travel; Melanie Weiner; Gail Worley; and Marcia Zellers at MTV OnLine. An extra round of applause goes out to Greg Fasolino and Judy McGuire for service above and beyond the call of duty.

A few people could only contribute off the record, and my thanks go out to them as well. Ditto for my pals and colleagues who, for professional reasons, couldn't cooperate, but didn't let my decision to write this book interefere with the rest of our relationship.

Without my agent, Dave Dunton, and his lovely wife, Regina Joskow Dunton, someone else might have written this book. Likewise, without Jim Fitzgerald, Deanna Mills, Rachael Woodruff, and all the fine folks at St. Martin's Press, a different entity would've published it. I'm pretty darned happy things turned out the way they did.

I am blessed with the most wonderful circle of friends, who are a source of constant joy to me. Extra special kudos to my parents and my brother for all their love and kindness over the past three decades. Your support and encouragement are deeply appreciated.

My roommate, Barbara Mitchell ("Queen of Darkness"), was an unwavering fount of inspiration, information, and motivation throughout this entire project. *Muchas gracias* from Señor El Toro.

This book is dedicated to the memory of Robert Penland, who taught me that all music is valid, and to Ann-Margret, "because writing a book is the hardest thing in the world."

BIG-TOP TRICKS: AN INTRODUCTION TO MARILYN MANSON

ELSEWHERE IN THIS BOOK you'll see a brief account of my first in-person encounter with Marilyn Manson. It's cut pretty short, but don't grudge the lost details; a longer one would serve no better. Though I've told and retold the story since that night two and a half years ago, no version has captured what really hit me. They say you never see the bullet that has your name on it, but this one came from so far out of nowhere that I didn't even hear it whistle until it was right between my eyes.

So what *did* really hit me? Put yourself where I was: a Carolina roadhouse called Ziggy's Tavern on a cold spring night in 1995. Wind rattles the plywood-and-plastic walls and you're perched uncomfortably on a hardwood bar stool, shivering. The band is two hours late (cops are reading them chapter and verse of the local ordinances on "public homa-sek-shul activity," but you don't know that . . .), you didn't really like their video or their CD, and you're wondering how in Hades your roommates ever talked you into this. Here's what I wrote then:

About 11:30 the houselights die and are replaced by a red pulsing glow from the stage, dry-ice fog coils around the amps; a tape begins to play, sound effects, snips of dialogue, distorted voices. Four figures walk on-stage and take their positions, quick about it, alertly watching stage left. It'll come from there, whatever it is. . . . It comes creeping into the red light, a twisted, crabbed shape, its shadow black and clutching as Nos-feratu's. Atavistic fear and awe grab my breath; can't help it, the shape in the smoke is archetypal Bad Thing, like a tree in the haunted forest. Slowly, spiderlike, all long legs and fingers and long lifeless hair, it makes its way to the mike stand. The kids are howling, mesmerized. It wraps its grip around the stand and stares with inhuman colorless eyes; yanks the stand toward itself with sudden violence and the band crashes into the huge discordant chime of 'Organ Grinder.' Holy shit. I remember to breathe. The Reverend Mr. Manson can sure as hell make an entrance. (I've forgotten I'm cold).

"Um, yeah," you say, "they used colored lights and smoke and you fell in love. Cripes, take her to see *Phantom of the Opera* and she'd probably have a grand-mal seizure." It's not quite that simple. They deployed these plain theatrics with the surest hand, absolutely certain of their shape; they reduced stage magic to its absolute basics—fire, smoke, shadows. Manson was viscerally engaged in his performance yet never without a sense of what his long, witchy silhouette looked like. The show's centerpiece was a fire set in a metal lunchbox, with Manson prowling around it, coaxing the flames upward with his fingers. I swear I didn't breathe once while it burned, a breathtakingly pure ritual, invoking voodoo revenge and the noninnocence of child-hood with laser intensity. It was the perfect accompaniment and equivalent to the music: hard, funny, scary rock and roll, full of rage and intelligence and deep disturbance. It just clobbered me. I knew in my bones that this was much more than it pretended to be; sleight of hand as a smoke screen for true spell casting. A cheap, painted sideshow that was home to real freaks and real wizards. I didn't know that night that their original name had been Marilyn Manson and the Spooky Kids, but if you'd told me I wouldn't have been surprised.

Those two and a half years have drawn a long road between there and here. Marilyn Manson's stage show is grander now, the grubby little bars are far behind them, and though authorities still turn out to stop their show, they're more likely to be backed by a state governor or a nationwide televangelist than the county sheriff. But at the core of them there's still that sense of what can be done inside people with the right combination of music and drama: the gift, as David Bowie called it, of sound and vision. And there's still more to them than meets the eye.

It's inside people, in fact, that Marilyn Manson do their best work. Don't be fooled by the stained glass and snow machines of the "Antichrist Superstar" tour, or whatever spectacle they'll use on the next one; they're still aiming at the same spot in your head as they were with dry ice and lunchbox fires. Not to make you go "ooh, wow" but to wake you up, to surprise you into thinking about what you see. They've progressed from the adolescent venom of the Spooky Kids days, when to expose and blast the failings of the adult world was goal enough, to a mature and focused assault on what Manson pictures as the string puller behind those adult failings: blind religious faith. And the goal of this assault is not (as the evangelicals fear) to convert you to Satan, but to make you see that blind faith of any kind—in God or Satan or even in Manson himself—is a trap, and that belief in yourself is the only source of strength. Which is the core of all true magick.

Do I have more belief in myself since I ran away with this circus? Most certainly. In the time that my roommates and I have been traveling to Manson shows, I've done things I wouldn't have thought me capable of. I've fought tooth and nail to hold my spot in the mosh pit; walked up to TV cameras and microphones to plead the band's, and my fellow Spooks', case when the censors started to close in; traveled hundreds of miles, made friends with strangers, argued with pastors, found needed things in totally strange cities, conquered one genuine lifelong phobia. (In fact, given a chance to actually talk to Manson, I didn't even lose my voice—try *that* for a test of self-possession.) And the heart-opening realization of just how much guilt and self-doubt had been ground into me by my Catholic upbringing—which I might have ended up spending hundreds of dollars and hours on a therapist's couch to reach—came to me on the barricade of Manson's April show in Winston-Salem, North Carolina. Only rock and roll, huh? I think not.

I've been lucky enough to attend shows by some of the greatest showmen and wildcats in rock: Bowie, Prince, Cooper, Lux Interior, Iggy Pop. I've seen some brilliant performances, but I've never seen anything as determined to stun *and* educate as Marilyn Manson. My point is that I fell for this, and have stayed with this, because it is unique. Marilyn Manson has influences by the handful but transcends them all. Like any well-constructed spell it weaves disparate elements, pulled from everywhere but carefully weighed for symbolism and resonance, into an integrated whole. I do sincerely believe that the full effect of Reverend Manson's "big science project" has yet to be seen or felt; it may be years yet or longer before we see the completion of it, in what the band does next or in whatever Manson chooses to do after rock and roll has served its purpose for him. But attempts to find labels for it will always fail, because there's no one thing that Marilyn Manson does.

Except magic.

Paula O'Keefe (==angelynx==)
September 27, 1997

MARILYN MANSON

⊙ΠΕ

ONCE UPON A TIME, long before the name Marilyn Manson sent shivers (of glee or revulsion, take your pick) up the spines of the world, a young couple lived twenty-five miles south of Akron, in the suburban dale of Canton, Ohio (pop. 84,161), in a bungalow located at 1420 NE Thirty-fifth Street. Hugh A. Warner was employed as a carpet salesman, and his wife Barbara was a licensed nurse. Potentially perfect parental material. And sure enough, on January 5, 1969, Barbara brought their only child, a son, into the world.

Despite his parents' best intentions, the wonder years of young Brian H. Warner didn't necessarily fall into *Leave It to Beaver* territory. "As a kid, I resented my father 'cause he wasn't around a lot," he would admit years later in an interview for *huH* magazine. Hugh also exhibited a violent temper, although Brian never claims to have been physically abused by his parents. Eventually, the father/son relationship would deepen, but at the time Brian couldn't always appreciate why his father behaved as he did.

One of several disturbing factors Brian would point to time and again when recalling his youth was that, as a soldier in the Vietnam War, his father had been sprayed with Agent Orange. This herbicide (including the contaminant dioxin) was used by the U.S. Army between 1965 and 1970 as a highly effective means of removing forest cover and destroying enemy crops. In subsequent years, however, a significant number of birth defects were detected in children of Vietnamese families who'd been exposed to Agent Orange; later, returning American veterans also began reporting high incidences of cancer and birth defects.

The government launched a variety of studies to examine the veracity of these claims and analyze the results. Both Hugh and Brian took part in one such research project. "At an early age I had to go to a lot of government testing to see if anything was wrong with me," he told *huH*. But no specific conclusions regarding a correlation between Agent Orange and any ill health—mental or physical—in the men of the Warner family were ever reached. Findings supported the government's claim that no link existed between exposure to Agent Orange and the aforementioned conditions (although in 1984, a new ten-year study, the Agent Orange Project, set about reexamining the controversy); many scientists feel that the neuropsychological effects of exposure to such herbicides are minimal (with the exception of Hodgkin's disease). Regardless, the testing presumably exerted an influence on Brian's developing psyche, sowing the seeds of distrust of political leaders that would continue to flourish.

As a result of his father's frequent absence, Brian stuck closer to Barbara. But she didn't exactly keep him tied to her apron strings. "I had a weird relationship with my mom as a kid because it was kind of abusive—but on my part," he admitted in *Rolling Stone*. "I wish I could go back and change the way I treated my mom because I used to be really rude to her, and she didn't really have any kind of control over me."

In 1974, the Warners elected to enroll Brian at Heritage Christian School, a private Catholic institution, rather than his local public elementary one. The family wasn't especially religious; they simply wanted to provide Brian with the best education possible. They couldn't have imagined the impact his prolonged tenure under Christian tutelage, which continued until tenth grade, would have on his life. "I'm glad I sent him to that school because of the educational value," Hugh once admitted in *Rolling Stone*. "But if I knew the result would be the demise of the rest of his morality that happened, I would never have done it."

From the outset, Brian was unhappy. "I cried a lot because I didn't want to be there," he admitted to future crony Veronica Kirchoff. "I didn't like to take naps, and I used to get in fights with all the girls." Yet he wasn't completely oblivious of his studies. "I received a good education, but in everything, even in math courses, they inserted morals and religious oppression," said Brian to *Alternative Press.* "Obviously that was the point of the school. That wasn't really the point of my parents sending me there—they wanted me to get a good education, but I received all of this extra baggage along with it."

Day in, day out, his teachers reiterated the wrath of God and the imminent Second Coming. "If I have to think back and pick the thing that I was afraid of the most, it was the end of the world, it was the coming of the apocalypse and the Antichrist. That was something that I stayed up every night and crying and just being completely afraid of." He fully recognized that, in the eyes of God and the world, he was a sinner, and therefore damned to hell if he didn't repent and beg forgiveness. But that's what made things worse: "I liked being a sinner."

With the end of the world (and probably algebra, too) weighing heavy on his mind, the release of sleep rarely came easily to Brian. And according to Barbara, a thwarted break-in at the family home when Brian was eight or nine, during the course of which the intruder attempted using a pillow to smother the child in his slumber, compounded this condition. Although the victim claims he doesn't remember the incident at all (and the conventional rule in first aid is that brain damage sets in within fifteen minutes of oxygen deprivation), even subconscious recollection of the incident was undoubtedly troubling to the boy. Eventually, he developed a habit of dozing off with the television on as a remedy for his fear of turning out the lights, a practice that he continues to this day.

His displeasure with the harsh realities of daily life and bleak future drove Brian further into his imagination. "From an early age, I wanted so much to see or experience something that wasn't normal," he said in *Rolling Stone*. His mother would try to discourage him from cursing by warning that the devil would come for him in his sleep. Brian waited up for him like other youngsters keep a vigil for Santa Claus. "I used to get excited because I really wanted it to happen. I was never afraid of what was under the bed. I wanted it. I wanted it more than anything."

Not surprisingly, he began to develop a penchant for fantasy that manifested itself in a variety of ways, including a fascination with role-playing games like Dungeons & Dragons. Contrasted with the heady consequences of the Second Coming of Christ, the cutthroat world of wizards, knights, and demons offered some welcome release. But his imagination didn't stop there. "Escapism was what it was about for me, because I didn't really like, and wasn't, the person that I wanted to be in the real world. So I was the person I wanted to be in my own head."

The person he had to be in the halls at school, however, wasn't nearly so fantastic. Like all students, Brian had to wear a uniform, keep his hair cut short, and was adamantly discouraged from listening to "the devil's music," rock and roll. But the authorities' efforts to enforce that last stricture only pointed him in the very direction from which they sought to avert him. "All the music that I found was through sermons on 'These Are the Things You Shouldn't Listen To.'" David Bowie was derided for promoting deviant sexuality; KISS, Alice Cooper, and Black Sabbath fell under fire for their presumed allegiance to Satan; like many others, Electric Light Orchestra and Black Oak Arkansas were held up as examples of the evils of backward masking (the subtleties of which, in retrospect, seemed to have shaped his aesthetic).

"And they'd show you pictures of the bands," he recalled in *Rolling Stone*, "and I was like, 'I like this. This is what I want.'"

That passion for rock music didn't help his popularity on any front. At school, his teachers punished him for his listening habits. "One time we got to bring our own music to sing and I brought AC/DC's *Highway to Hell*," he told *Details*. "I got kicked out of class." And although his parents even drove him to his first KISS concert ("My dad dressed up like KISS"), the senior Warners apparently weren't entirely devoid of reservations concerning their son's listening habits. "When I first bought *Piece of Mind*, my mother tried to return it because she thought it was too Satanic," he told *Guitar World*. "She took it back to the record store because she didn't want me to listen to it." Rest assured, Mrs. Warner, that although Iron Maiden has sung about the Antichrist, they aren't practicing Satanists.

Since he couldn't fit in with his classmates at Heritage, he tried to mix with the public school students, who assumed that, because of where he was enrolled, he was a spoiled sissy. To compound the situation, Brian was a skinny kid, thus making him an easy target. Plus he was prone to illness; in addition to multiple bouts with pneumonia, he also told *Guitar School* that he'd had polyps removed from his rectum (à la former president Ronald Reagan). "I had to have my urethra enlarged because the hole through which I urinate wasn't large enough to accommodate the stream I was projecting," he continued. "I had an allergic reaction to antibiotics once and I almost died."

Fortunately, other kids at Heritage didn't enjoy such permissive home environments, and enterprising Brian saw an opportunity in their predicament. "I started going to the record store and buying, like a W.A.S.P. record for seven bucks, and selling it for, like, twenty bucks to some kid whose parents wouldn't let him go to record stores," he told *Rolling Stone*. But his mischief didn't end there. Since the students were on an honor system, and didn't actually have locks on their lockers, he'd return later in the day to where his customer had stashed the record and reclaim it, knowing full well they couldn't confront him with the trespass unless they incriminated themselves.

But Brian wasn't looking toward a career in music sales. Inspired by his heroes, he knew there were bigger fish to fry. "As a kid, I always thought, 'What am I gonna be when I grow up?' " he recalls. "And I knew what I wanted to be was an actor or a singer, a writer or an entertainer. I didn't want to have a real job, where I had to work at manual labor." He made his first steps in that direction by recording tapes of original material at home and selling them to his classmates. The programs were a bizarre mix of crank calls, twisted comedy, and songs on such pertinent topics as farts, jerking off, and assorted sexual fantasies. He also began penning his own primitive cartoon humor zine, inspired by titles like *Mad* and *Cracked*.

The sexual content on Brian's cassette jams undoubtedly seemed advanced considering his age and popularity. According to one anecdote he's shared occasionally, that might be due in part to being pressured by another, older boy to engage in "prison games" while still around the age of eight. Brian had a next-door neighbor who was twelve or thirteen at the time. In the afternoons, Brian would go over to watch the Japanese sci-fi television show *Ultraman*. "One day, he told me, 'Let's play like we're in prison, and we're stranded, and take off all your clothes.' We took off all of our clothes, and we're in this closet, and he's molesting me. It may have been more of a harmless childhood thing. I went home and I told my parents, and they didn't believe it, wouldn't acknowledge it, said that I was lying," Brian told *Seconds*.

But mostly children act out what they learn at home. Our hero might not have been afraid of whatever bogeymen lurked under his bed, but the monster in his grandparents' basement would be a primary bugbear for the rest of his life.

THE DETAILS CHANGE EVERY time he recounts the story now, but the composite version goes something like this. Brian's paternal grandfather Jack, a truck driver, had cancer, and as a consequence had undergone a tracheotomy. "He couldn't speak, just kind of barked in gravelly grunts," he told Jon Pecorelli in *Alternative Press*. "He spent most of his time in the basement where he had these train sets and what we discovered when we were about twelve is that whenever he'd turn the trains on he was always masturbating, heavily, to all these real extreme fetish mags, like enema mags and gay porno." Alternate versions of this tale expand Grandpa Jack's collection of accoutrements to include "bestiality porn and dildos and women's lingerie."

This was essentially his formal introduction to sex, and though it wouldn't completely take shape for a while, his overall impression was very different from the version represented in the pages of *Pent-*

house or *Playboy*. "To me, sex was ugly and still is—[it's] about fucking pigs and putting douche bags up your ass," he shared in *Paper*. Not that he considered these gruesome associations particularly negative, but he knew they didn't fall within the carefully prescribed parameters of normal adolescent desire.

The impact of his discovery manifested itself in several ways. "I used to take pictures of naked women, and I would cut out just their sex organs," he told *Rolling Stone*. "And I started having really violent dreams that I was doing that to real people."

Fortunately, Brian's initial forays into the mysteries of sex were as normal as those of most teenagers. According to *Details*, he'd procured his first smooch from "a minister's daughter named Jill Tucker who had whitish blond hair and buckteeth. I liked her a lot, but even in the third grade I saw that her being a minister's daughter would prove a problem for me."

Then at age sixteen, one October night our hero and a girl named Rita, "drunk on half a quart of Jim Beam whiskey" he'd stolen from his grandmother and hidden in a KISS thermos, snuck out under cover of darkness on to a baseball diamond. "And very similar to the scene in *Fast Times at Ridgemont High* where Jennifer Jason Leigh loses her virginity, so did I—in a fumbling attempt that lasted all of 30 seconds," he wrote in—of all things—a review of the Tom Petty boxed set for *huH* (it seems the song "American Girl" from 1976's *Tom Petty and the Heartbreakers* kept going through his head). Years later, he confessed to *Rolling Stone* he found the setting "kind of ironic, because I hate sports." (It is fair to assume then that Brian rarely visited the Pro Football Hall of Fame, Canton's biggest tourist attraction.)

Another important discovery he made around this time was the world of illicit drugs. "I went over to this kid's house to stay for the weekend and his brother pulled up in a GTO," he recalls. "He got out of the car and he instantly started firing off a pistol into the sky, which I knew meant that I was in for an interesting weekend. He had this special party room that was real dark with Lava lamps and all these posters of Grim Reapers and skulls. He broke out a bong and we started smoking marijuana while listening to Ozzy Osbourne. Then he talked me into drinking the bongwater. I got sick for like a week."

Meanwhile, he was reaching the end of his rope with Catholic school. The scheduled date for Armageddon had passed with nary a fanfare, and it was becoming apparent to Brian that the emperor wore no clothes. "The turning point was [when] they were preaching a lot of doom to the kids in the school around 1984, and saying it was gonna be the end of the world. The Antichrist was coming . . . electronic sensors in grocery stores were gonna be used to read the number of the beast off of kids' hands, and so on and so forth. And when 1985 came around, and I stopped having nightmares because I was terrified to fall asleep every night, I realized that I was being lied to, and that there was no reason to be buying into this, and I started searching for other truths, reading a lot, experiencing life. Experiencing everything that I was told not to. Because I wanted to know why they were trying to keep me away from it.

"Growing up I was always interested in finding out the other side of the story; why people don't like things," he shared in *Flipside*. "I always kind of gravitated to things that people don't like. I want to find out why they don't like them, because I know people don't like me and that doesn't necessarily mean that I'm a bad person. It's all according to your perspective."

His entertaining antics had brought him respect—or at least attention—from his peers, but Brian's propensity to stir up trouble also reflected a more subversive nature. Finally, he figured out a way to escape his academic prison for good. "It was an ultimatum situation where I wanted to get kicked out," he told the fanzine *Gear*. "I got caught for a bunch of different things, one of which was stealing money out of girls' purses during prayer, which I thought was poetic, because obviously TV evangelists steal money out of girls' purses during prayer also, in their own way."

Years later, in a "homecoming" article published by the *Repository*, a daily paper in Canton, several of Brian's old classmates shared their impressions of him. "[He was] just average," claimed Neil Ruble, a classmate from Heritage who'd ridden the bus with him all through elementary school up to the tenth grade (when they both returned to the public school system). "He's always been really skinny like a twig. I would go over to his house and we'd listen to records together, stuff like Queensryche, Iron Maiden, lots of Judas Priest. I was more into it than he was. He used to play the drums a little bit, too. I didn't even know he sang.

"Before [Brian] left, he had real long hair," added Ruble. "I thought he was just one of these bozos who was going to be in a band. I didn't think he really had anything going for him [musically] and maybe he doesn't. Maybe he just got lucky."

Jeff Seeman (who nowadays claims to be "an avid fan of Marilyn Manson's music") went to school with Brian at GlenOak. "He wasn't like this," he told the *Repository*, "but he was definitely unusual."

In a more permissive educational environment, Brian was free to study art (he took to re-creating Iron Maiden album artwork) and creative writing. The latter "was the only thing that made going to school worth it," he admitted to *Gear*. "I think maybe even part of some of the things I wrote in high school later transformed into Marilyn Manson songs. At least ideas of pieces."

Entering the public school system so late in the composition of the social pecking order, Brian had trouble making friends. " 'I didn't really have anyone that I could have called a best friend," he said in the *Times Leader*. "So I ended up spending a lot of time on my own, and developing a chip on my shoulder which I've taken out later in life."

Finding a girlfriend was an even more daunting problem. Frustration simmered over into a streak of misogyny. Senior year, he became fixated on one of the most popular girls at GlenOak. "I kept trying to go out with her because I was the most unpopular person in school," he admitted in *Rolling Stone*. Finally, she acquiesced, but he didn't know what exactly to do with her on their date. "I wasn't even going to try and kiss her because I was afraid to do the wrong thing." They returned to his parents' place to discover Mr. and Mrs. Warner out for the evening. "She was, like, this pristine, popular girl, and the minute she got to my house, she had her clothes off and just, you know, wanted to fuck. Then the next day she didn't even talk to me." He likened the event to learning his grandfather's secret, as "a moment of having my idea of what something was supposed to be destroyed."

Two

SHORTLY AFTER BRIAN COMPLETED his education at GlenOak High School back in Ohio ("I ended up graduating with not a lot of friends," he told *Flipside*), Hugh Warner accepted a new sales job offer that took the family from their cozy Midwest environs to a wholly new locale: southern Florida. Specifically, first to Pompano Beach, and later, the burg where Brian resided throughout the early years of the band that would become Marilyn Manson: Boca Raton. The latter had been developed by architect Addison Mizner in the 1920s, but was barely out of the developmental stages when the Great Depression hit the Sunshine State. Boca Raton continued to sprout up slowly over the course of the next fifty years, without ever producing the sort of localized town center that traditionally anchors a community. What did lend Boca Raton a certain uniformity was the look of the buildings, marked by a strong Spanish-revival influence, typically done in burnt sienna or pink, with barrel tile roofs, often featuring iron balconies or canopies.

Brian lived with his parents, but apparently managed to keep out of too much trouble. The only easily uncovered blot on the otherwise untarnished record of his late teens involves a minor car accident, very shortly after the family left Ohio, on August 28, 1988. While driving his mother's Cadillac El Dorado, traveling north on a cloudy day, he was hit in the right front corner by what the police report comically refers to as "a phantom vehicle," resulting in an estimated five hundred dollars in damages. Warner, who'd been cruising along at a respectful thirty-five miles per hour in a thirty-five zone, wasn't held responsible.

Evidence offered up in later years suggests that while Brian continued to reside under the same roof as his folks, the situation wasn't always exactly rosy. In an interview conducted in 1994 for an unfinished television documentary on youth culture, Warner (by then very much established in his Marilyn Manson persona) observed that one source of conflicts between parents and children was the older generation recognizing too much of themselves in their offspring. "They see the things their kids are doing, and they know that that's stuff that they did, or want to do now. And there's a little bit of envy there, because they can't live that life anymore. And I think that resentment often informs their attitude in how they treat their kids. That's what I felt that I was experiencing a lot when I was around eighteen, was that I got a lot of shit about 'get a job, you're a loser' because my dad would work a twelve-hour day, and see that I'm just sitting around the house."

Slowly but surely, the junior Warner did begin to exhibit a modicum of initiative, seeking out entry-level gigs writing about music for two local publications. "He wrote reviews and entertainment columns [for magazines], one of which was called *Tonight, Today* and the other one was called *25th Parallel*," recalls Scott Mitchell, a local musician who would become very important to Warner over the course of the next six years. Both publications are now defunct. "And when he worked at *25th Parallel*, he did a lot, but they never paid him," continues Mitchell. "He wrote a lot of columns under different names."

As is the case in most geographic regions, South Florida boasted a distinctive musical sound. But those bands stood in marked contrast to the sunny disposition that still permeates this tourist destination. The loud, abrasive sound—dubbed "death metal"—drew on such well-known influences as the increasingly popular Metallica (who had just broken into the mainstream in 1988 with the ominous ballad "One"), crossed with lesser-known acts such as Slayer, Venom, and European cult favorites Celtic Frost. Early proponents of the distinctly regional sound included the bands Death (from Orlando) and Obituary (nee Xecutioner, from Tampa). Later groups such as Deicide, Cannibal Corpse, Raped Ape, Morbid Angel, and Malevolent Creation would join their ranks. Their songs dealt with such extreme and disquieting topics as dismemberment, necrophilia, and murder.

"Death metalers embrace a sense of white-trash rejection, then magnify it a million times," noted *Details* magazine in 1995. But not all bands in the South Florida scene fell under the death metal banner, even the most shocking ones. The Genitorturers' live show, which involves enemas, hot wax sessions, simulated oral sex, piercing, and whipping, often generated far more attention than their music. But even in this environment, Warner would later claim that very few people took his ideas, or his band, seriously. "The music scene's a little weird down there," he confessed to *Seconds* when asked if he felt a camaraderie with other groups from his neck of the woods. "Some of the bands are together but we started out on our own and nobody every wanted to help us. A lot of the more technical rock bands never gave us any respect and said that our music was shitty and they didn't like us."

BUT MARILYN MANSON WEREN'T going to spring fully formed solely from the skull of Brian Warner, and while his personality was taking shape in Ohio and Florida, another key player was growing up in West Orange, in New Jersey. "I've been learning instruments since I was a little kid," says the man now known as Scott Mitchell. He started out on flute around the age of eight, then quickly moved on to snare drum a few years later. "And we had a piano in my home, which I dabbled with a little bit. I didn't really learn it too well."

His family moved to Florida in 1980, and Scott attended school in Coral Springs. Around the time that puberty had started to roll in, he picked up his first guitar. "I got a really small, cheap [one] from my cousin when I was thirteen or fourteen, and I took a year of guitar in high school, and that's where I first started learning and playing. At the time, I was into the Cars and the Cure, punk and new wave, and British music. Everybody else in my guitar class was into Iron Maiden and Black Sabbath and Jimi Hendrix. That's all stuff that I've grown to love, but they liked it before I did. I was like the art fag in the class. But I didn't care, I just liked learning the guitar."

What he didn't like, however, was attending classes. "I dropped out of high school because I hated it, and got a GED [general equivalency diploma]. I was pretty pissed that a three-hour test was the equivalent of four years in that school. But then I went to the Art Institute of Fort Lauderdale, in 1986, and I graduated in '88." His concentrations were in advertising design and marketing, two areas that ironically would remain very important to him, even though his career was leading him far away from their traditional applications.

Sometime in late 1989, Mitchell and Brian Warner were introduced at a party. ("Where else?" he laughs loudly. "At a library, looking up Kant and Kierkegaard?") "I thought he was a big geek," recalls Mitchell. "He used to wear these fluffy shirts with interesting prints, and big creeper shoes with the thick soles, and black jeans and rings, and he had long, light brown hair."

Perhaps his fashion sense left something to be desired, but Brian Warner's muse had already begun to emerge, although his initial inclination to pursue a career in writing didn't last long. "I was writing short stories and verse that could or could not be put into song form," he told *Alternative Press*. "It wasn't really important to me at the time, I was just expressing some ideas." But being a music journalist, on the other hand, was already beginning to cramp his style. "I found out really quickly that I couldn't express my voice in the medium that I was working in. And after meeting different performers and hearing what they had to say, a lot of the shallowness that takes place in music, I realized that a lot of musicians are just that—musicians. They don't really care to have a message or be anything other than that. It inspired me to want to do better and make a difference."

At the time, Scott Mitchell was already in another band (his latest of several), called India Loves You. "It was pretty psychedelic, and almost folky," he explains. "I was working with a girl named Cindy Deats, who has a band called Backwash now. And I had gotten a drum machine, and a four-track, to do recording with. I had made up a bunch of songs on my own, and started working with Cindy, just because I was uncomfortable with singing. I wanted somebody else to sing and write lyrics. It was just me and her. We weren't going for any particular sound, we were just having fun. And it was kind of weird and psychedelic, but it was structured." Which wasn't to say they aspired to be the new Phish; "It wasn't like a jam band situation, because I don't like that stuff. We did that for about a year, a year and a half maybe."

Brian Warner needed a collaborator to provide music for his verses to turn them into songs; Mitchell seemed suitable, and the two began to work together. "He had never been in a band before, and had no musical experience. He didn't play anything, he just wrote . . . weird poems, and I liked what he wrote, so I thought he could do that. He couldn't really sing, but he didn't have to, because we were doing experimental mixtures of industrial and basic rock. It was just a weird meld of styles, because we weren't shooting for anything in particular. I had a weird background, it wasn't like I was a metalhead or a techno geek or anything, I just liked all the new stuff that I was listening to. So I had the drum machine and regular guitars and distorted vocals. And a lot of people had never heard anything like this before. And I never thought it would go anywhere."

As the two began writing together, India Loves You fell by the wayside, and Mitchell stopped working with Deats. "There was actually a day, after I met Brian, that the two of them were sitting in my room together, and Brian was insisting that I decide who I was going to work with. I didn't think about it like I could've worked with both, because he was being a little demanding. I should've taken note of that at that time. 'I know it looks like a wolf, but it may not be,' " he wisecracks. "[Brian] was kind of insistent. He had convinced me to get a drum machine, which was good, and he exposed me to earlier forms of industrial music. And we had a good idea going, so I decided to work with him, and Cindy kind of went her own way."

The "good idea" to which Mitchell refers was going to do just as much as, if not more than, the music to help establish their band. They'd decided to dub their fledgling outfit Marilyn Manson, an homage to the beloved Hollywood sexpot and America's most infamous serial killer. But the concepts behind that moniker ran much deeper than just a simple juxtaposition of two famous names. "I watch a lot of talk shows, and I was struck by how they lumped together Hollywood starlets with serial killers, just bringing everything to the same sensational level," Warner explained to the *Sun-Sentinel* newspaper in July of 1994. "But Monroe had a dark side with her drugs and depressions, and Manson had a true message and charisma for his followers, so it's not all black and white."

They were the ultimate in opposites. But more importantly, the combination of the two captured some of the mass media contradictions that he felt young people were bombarded with twenty-four hours a day. "I thought that those two—positive/negative, male/female, good/evil, beauty/ugliness—created the perfect dichotomy of everything I wanted to represent," he admitted in *XS* magazine. Eventually, he also began to appreciate that several historical philosophers had already explored these ideas from a more academic perspective. On at least one early occasion, he likened the combination of names and identities to "the way that a philosopher like Hegel had created his thesis of juxtaposition of diametrically opposed archetypes."

Although for years Warner's version of the birth of Marilyn Manson has him coming up with the idea first, and then meeting Mitchell, the guitarist claims that isn't the case. "It was not his idea," he asserts. "We came up with it together." Regardless, the concept didn't just stop at the band name. All the players over the next six years would adopt names that paired the first name of a female sex symbol with the last name of a serial killer. Scott Mitchell became Daisy Berkowitz, while Brian Warner adopted the name Marilyn Manson for himself. Given the derivation, the fuss surrounding Warner's decision to adopt the name Marilyn Manson seems understandable.

Fittingly, Charles Manson had also been born in Ohio, but his own upbringing was a mite more tumultuous than Brian Warner's. He was born on November 12, 1934, in Cincinnati; his birth certificate lists him simply as "No Name Maddox." His mother was a sixteen-year-old prostitute named Kathleen Maddox. After his mom and uncle were packed off to prison to serve time for robbing a gas station, young Charles was sent to live with a nasty aunt and her even crueler husband, who taunted him, calling him a sissy. In an attempt to spur the boy to "act like a man," the uncle dressed him in girl's clothes for his first day of school. When Kathleen was released from jail and reclaimed him, things didn't exactly look up for the lad; on one occasion his mother purportedly swapped the child to a barmaid in exchange for a pitcher of beer.

In 1947, Kathleen Maddox tried to unload her son into the foster care system, but nobody would take him. He ran away and hit the road at around the age of twelve, committing robberies and stealing cars. Within a year he was caught and sentenced to three years in reform school. Manson claims that one of his guards encouraged the other boys to rape and torture him while the guard stood by and watched, masturbating. In 1951 Manson and two pals escaped, stealing cars and ending up in Utah. This time the consequences proved more severe, and he pulled time in a federal prison for driving stolen cars across state lines. After he raped another inmate at razor point, Manson was classified as "dangerous" and sent to an even more secure facility. Yet he quickly conned the parole board and was released in 1954. A series of further stints in and out of prison culminated in an eventual release in 1967.

Charles gravitated to San Francisco's Haight-Ashbury. It was here that the charismatic figure began to acquire the followers that would compose his sinister "Family." The group, which had about fifty members at its peak, was sometimes affiliated with the Church of Satan and the notorious Process Church. A series of murders were eventually linked to the Manson Family, but their most prolific month was in 1969, when the group killed at least nine people in Southern California. In 1970, Manson went to trial for the seven Tate-LaBianca murders; among the victims in that slaying were starlet Sharon Tate, of *Valley of the Dolls* renown, pregnant at the time. As Manson's death sentence was announced, the body of his attorney, Ronald Hughes, was discovered rotting, after a car ride with two

Family members. (Charles Manson still comes up for parole every few years, but the swastika carved into his forehead tends to send the wrong kind of message to the parole board.)

Scott Mitchell's new handle, Daisy Berkowitz, was calculated to be just as inflammatory as Marilyn Manson. The first component was innocent enough, a nod to the Daisy Duke character (she of the short shorts) on the television show *The Dukes of Hazzard*. But the second portion alluded to David Berkowitz, alias "Son of Sam," a murderer who'd held the typically unflappable denizens of New York City in the grip of fear for thirteen months, beginning in July of 1976. Berkowitz's deadly spree kicked off when two women in a parked car were shot—one fatally—by an unseen assailant. Months later another fatal shooting was matched to this first one. After a third incident in a similar fashion the following month, police knew they had a serial killer on their hands. Initially he was tagged "the .44-caliber killer," "Mr. 44," and, most endearingly, "Mister Monster." (Though Mitchell would never adopt any of these nicknames himself, during the early years of the band he was sometimes associated with the real Berkowitz's self-designed monogram—a large X quartered with male and female symbols, an S, and a cross.)

But the shootings continued unabated. After a double homicide in April of the following year, the police found a crude note in which the killer referred to himself as the "Son of Sam." After the first letter, more and more missives from the killer continued to surface (some going to newspaper columnist Jimmy Breslin), all ominous, and warning of more carnage to come. The police finally tracked down the Son of Sam after a check of parking tickets that were issued near the final homicide. The chubby, innocuous-looking Berkowitz claimed his neighbor's Labrador retriever was transmitting homicidal commands to him. Berkowitz was a virgin at his arrest and at first seemed to be acting out hostility toward all the women who'd rejected him. (Later reports have him being part of a nationwide Satanic ring, but that's still up for debate.)

Not surprisingly, the desired effect of the band's names missed the mark to a certain degree; in most coverage, the focus tended to shift to the mass murderer surnames, rather than the dichotomy of light and dark represented by the two halves. Marilyn Manson and his cohorts quickly learned to speak articulately on the topic. "I look on the serial killers cynically, more tongue-in-cheek," Manson told *Seconds* in an early interview. "It's basically everybody's fear of death that fascinates them with serial killers. America makes them into heroes. America complains that kids are idolizing them, but they don't have anyone to play with." Despite the vast pantheon of fascinating figures in the annals of bloodletters and badmen, Manson never claimed to harbor a particular affinity for or aversion to any specific killer. "I'm not repulsed by anyone other than the people who later cop out and say they're born again and that they want forgiveness for their crimes," he insisted. "I think that if someone commits a crime they need to be responsible for it."

As far as Manson was concerned, differentiating between serial killers and soldiers in a war (including his own father, who'd seen combat action in Vietnam) was hypocritical. "They want to make someone in war into a hero, but they want to make a serial killer into a criminal," he told *Flipside*. "It's just a popularity contest; to me, it's all the same thing. Nobody is innocent, so you can't say somebody has killed innocent people. It's nature. Everything dies and it's nobody's fault. It's not right or wrong, it just is. You can't do anything about it."

Disappointingly, his opinions on Marilyn Monroe were rarely as sharp. On the other hand, he was also pressed to share them far less frequently, even though the starlet's name was just as inextricably linked to her identity as the murderer's was to his own. Early on Marilyn Manson admitted that he'd seen few of the actress's films, and didn't admire her for her thespian capabilities. He was more concerned with her prestigious status as a sex icon, and had trouble imagining the landscape of popular culture had she never existed. "I don't think there's anyone that could compare to Marilyn Monroe for me as far as that kind of identity," he told *Seconds*, adding that only S and M pinup girl Betty Page had ever exerted as much of an attraction for him.

Six years later, looking back on the decision to become Marilyn Manson, the singer had become much more reflective, and able to offer an increasingly refined take on the many levels on which his name could be considered. "It was symbolic to kind of shed the skin of my past—people refer to your given name as your Christian name—so there's symbolism there," he admitted to Paul Semel in an interview for *huH.* "And it was also the idea that show business is so fake that I wanted to pick a name that was as fake as it could be, so it would be realer than anything else because it acknowledges itself as being fake. Marilyn Monroe itself was a fake name, and Charles Manson was not his born name either, so I thought that was an exciting irony for me."

With Berkowitz as lead guitarist and Manson on vocals, the duo set out to recruit a full band. They emerged at the end of 1989 as Marilyn Manson and the Spooky Kids. The pair were joined by Perry Pandrea, whom they dubbed Zsa Zsa Speck (an amalgamation of *Queen of Outer Space* star Zsa Zsa Gabor and student-nurse stalker Richard Speck) on keyboards, and Brian Tutunick, alias Olivia Newton-Bundy (Australian pop tart Olivia Newton-John and killer Ted Bundy), on bass. A Yamaha RX8 drum machine handled rhythm duties. Pandrea and Tutunick didn't last long, although the latter continued to work on the scene in a series of bands. He became the vocalist for L.U.N.G.S., which soon became Collapsing Lungs (who released an EP entitled *Colorblind* on Atlantic Records in 1994), and later reverted to a version of the first name, Lungs. Tutunick is currently a member of the outfit Nation of Fear.

Brad Stewart and Steven Bier Jr. replaced Bundy and Speck on bass and keyboards, respectively. Stewart was christened Gidget Gein, while Bier became Madonna Wayne Gacy. Once again, their new forenames were suitable showbiz ladies'. Gidget was the name of a fictitious swinging sixties California teenager portrayed by several starlets—including Sandra Dee and future Academy Award winner Sally Field—on the big and small screens. And Madonna was the singer/media sensation who'd already racked up seventeen hit singles by this time.

Likewise, their surnames acknowledged the legacy of two garish murderers. Ed Gein, the man who inspired the Alfred Hitchcock thriller *Psycho,* truly lived up to his reputation. After the death of his mother (a religious woman who warned against premarital sex, but permitted masturbation), Ed was left alone in the house. Although he'd always secretly longed to be a woman, the notion of castration proved too unsettling to him. Unready to commit to being a full-time female, he still sought out a method to change his gender on a part-time basis. He began by unearthing bodies from graves and using different parts of the deceaseds' anatomy as decoration: Skulls became decorative tops to bedposts; mobiles were fashioned from noses, lips, and labia. Not all of the organs were merely decorative; skullcaps were sensibly transformed into bowls and Gein often held up his pants with a belt made of nipples. But his real passion lay in dressing up and becoming the woman he'd always wanted to be. He would wear a vest that was complete with actual breasts, then strap on female genitalia over his cursed male organ.

However, Gein's heinous crimes didn't end with sexual perversion and the desecration of corpses. In 1954 he killed a woman named Mary Hogan, but although the police later found evidence of foul play, including a pool of blood and a spent cartridge, they failed to produce the woman's body. Three years later, another lass disappeared in a similar manner, and this time the authorities connected the disappearance to Gein. When they arrived at his house, they found the victim's heart in a saucepan, and a box of other organs lying in a box in the corner. Her headless corpse hung from the rafters, gutted, with the genitals cut out. In 1958, Gein was declared insane and institutionalized, and he died in 1984.

John Wayne Gacy's story also measured up to the other members of the murderous elite honored by the names of the new Manson family. Gacy was an outstanding member of his community, and a leader in the local Jaycees. Yet behind closed doors, the troubled closet homosexual would berate his own son with taunts of "sissy." In 1968, Gacy was arrested for pressuring a young male employee into gay sex acts. After having the boy beaten, Gacy pled guilty to sodomy. He was sentenced to ten years in prison, but was released a year and a half later. His first wife understandably chose to divorce him, but he soon remarried and moved into a middle-class suburb of Chicago. Gacy's pastime was dressing up as a circus clown and entertaining the neighborhood kids. He even met First Lady Rosalynn Carter in his guise of "Pogo the Clown," an encounter commemorated in an infamous photograph. But despite his outward veneer as a family man, Gacy's penchant for young boys soon brought him trouble with the law again. Accused of attempting to rape a boy, he was charged with disorderly conduct, yet the charges were dismissed after the boy blew off the court date.

Gacy committed his first murder in 1972. He often disguised himself as a cop; his modus operandi was to solicit young males, from the neighborhood or bus terminals, with his tastes alternating between students and street hustlers. After sex and torture, Gacy would bury his prey in the crawlspace under his house. After Gacy's second wife left him, he picked up the pace of his murderous activities. When police came to his house to question the fiend about the disappearance of a local youth, they noticed the stench of decaying flesh emanating from the floorboards. Upon inspection, the grounds of Gacy's house and yard yielded twenty-eight buried bodies, and five more were recovered nearby. Gacy subsequently enjoyed a successful career from jail as a painter, favoring macabre portraits of clowns, which have been purchased by celebrities including actor Johnny Depp, Lux Interior of psychobilly quartet the Cramps, and filmmaker John Waters.

Madonna Wayne Gacy had purportedly never touched an instrument before being recruited, but with his appreciation for socialism, nihilist philosopher Schopenhauer, and seminal punk quartet the Ramones, he certainly had the right spirit for the enterprise. "I'm not about musicians, I hate musicians," he decreed in an early interview with the *Gaston Gazette*. "I'm all about entertaining, you know. That's why I have more in common with a stripper than fucking Billy Joel. I'm more worried about entertaining than writing art and all that stupid shit. It's not about art at all, it's about giving something fun and putting on a show."

And put on shows they did. According to accounts of early performances, passed down among fans for years to come, from the word "go" Marilyn Manson gigs resembled nothing the likes of South Florida had seen before. A Lite Brite toy set up on stage boasted catchy slogans like "Anal Fun" and "Kill God." Manson would sometimes throw peanut-butter-and-jelly sandwiches into the crowd. The list of antics only grew with time, eventually including (on various and sundry occasions) caged or crucified women, a papier-mâché Cyclops, a blood-splattered Ronald McDonald, plenty of shredded Bibles, raw meat, and slide projectors. Nudity, arson, nothing was too taboo. Yet surprisingly, the authorities rarely interfered. "The closest we've ever come to being arrested was having a six-year-old kid in a cage on stage singing one of our songs, at the same time having a naked girl crucified to a cross," Manson told *Seconds*. "The kid was out of line of sight from the girl, but everybody else could see them both. I thought it was a weird little science project without actually breaking the law."

Charles Manson sound bites might mix with readings from timeless children's classics like *The Cat in the Hat*. Marilyn Manson might recite passages by his namesake Charles during shows, including one rant that was especially popular with the crowds: "I play music. People are affected by the music I play. That doesn't mean I direct traffic! That doesn't mean I put a knife in anyone's hand and tell 'em to go kill somebody!" Manson's own stage wear might be all stripes, or a woman's bathing suit, while Berkowitz also tended to cross-dress, in a blond wig and skirt, guitar slung low, like a member of the Runaways or one of Josie's Pussycats gone horribly wrong. Meanwhile, Madonna Wayne Gacy created a little booth labeled "Pogo's Playhouse" (having adopted Gacy's nickname as his own) for his keyboards.

Of course, rumors of the proceedings occasionally got twisted far beyond the truth. Jack Kearney, current owner of the Fort Lauderdale club where Marilyn Manson enjoyed many of their earliest shows, tried to set the record straight in *Rolling Stone* in June 1997: "People see what they want to see. Brian Warner is rock's Houdini. He had a girl named Terry tied to the cross and semi-naked at a show here, and when everybody left, [people] were saying she was totally naked and her throat was cut." But as another local eventually noted in *New Times*, "even performances that didn't feature naked women nailed to a cross, a child in a cage, or bloody animal body parts were still impressive and memorable."

Almost from their inception, the band also began to take advantage of Daisy's four-track to make self-packaged promotional tapes. Between their earliest incarnation and the appearance of the 1991 cassette entitled *After School Special*, they released at least three (and possibly a fourth, *Snuffy's VCR*) such documents in extremely limited editions (originals are now highly prized collector's items). The debut *Meat Beat Cleaver Beat* is falsely rumored to have featured contributions from Zsa Zsa Speck and Olivia Newton-Bundy, although just verifying a track listing has stymied even the most hard-core Marilyn Manson fans. *big black bus*, named after the method of transportation engaged by the original Manson Family, followed in the summer of 1990, and featured four songs: "White Knuckles," "My Monkey," "Strange Same Dogma," and "Red in My Head." The flip side comprised answering-machine messages. According to the liner notes, Manson and Daisy oversaw all the production. Although Gidget Gein was present at two of the three sessions, he made no discernible contributions to the creative process. Daisy handled keyboards, guitars, and drum programming duties, in addition to writing all the music, while Manson provided the lyrics. Engineered by "Graveyard" Ralph Cavallaro, the tape was recorded at the Sync Studios in Miami. Shortly thereafter, another tape appeared. Entitled *Grist-O-Line*, it featured four more songs: "Dune Buggy," "Cake and Sodomy," "Meat for a Queen," and "She's Not My Girlfriend."

Musically, the group had brewed up a sound that captured the same intention of many of the bands Manson and Berkowitz liked and admired: Black Sabbath, Dr. Hook, Alice Cooper, Iggy Pop, David Bowie, late Beatles, early Rolling Stones. But with the incorporation of samples and the pervasive element of Grand Guignol, much of the influence was more spiritual than musical. And while Manson wasn't a musician himself, his input into the compositions was still important. "He would have very rough ideas of sounds he wanted, or rhythms," says Scott Mitchell, who also acknowledges Manson's occasional melodic ideas. "He was groping for something he wanted to do. Which he's been doing ever since." Regardless, the making of the earliest tapes was a relatively painless affair.

Manson's biggest contribution (aside from his outrageous stage persona and fount of grisly ideas) was his lyrics. Many songs at this point featured lyrics that Manson had penned before hooking up with Berkowitz. Having read Lawrence Ferlinghetti and sixties Beat poets while still in his teens, Manson aspired to comment on the state of the world around him in his writings; despite his startling imagery, he wasn't interested in penning gloomy Gothic ramblings, and didn't consider his work poetry per se. "A lot of my lyrics are obtained from my childhood," he told the fanzine *M.E.A.T.*, "from people that I've met along the way, experiences that I've had. I just relate these things with music so that other people will be able to relate to them also. Yet most people will have to find their own interpretation of the lyrics. I just try to be honest—that's why our lyrics are sometimes more raw than what people might expect."

Given the combination of shocking elements at play in their act and music, Marilyn Manson and the Spooky Kids began to gain wider acclaim. Most notably, they landed a plum one-off gig with Nine Inch Nails on their summer tour of 1990, playing the foremost opening slot, before Meat Beat Manifesto and NiN. For a spell Manson would claim that this was his first meeting with Trent Reznor. But Scott Mitchell purports that he had already met the Nine Inch Nails frontman in his guise of Brian Warner, rock journalist, when he'd been assigned to do a story on NiN's breakout debut *Pretty Hate Machine*. In later years, Manson would come clean and admit he'd met Reznor in the manner Mitchell recalls. "He was actually one of the people that was encouraging to me, in the sense that we grew up in the same kind of environment, in the Midwest, and he seemed to be someone that made his dream happen." The two outcasts clicked on myriad levels, and the high-profile spot was only the first of many beneficial results to stem from their nascent friendship.

By the summer of 1990, the band had decided to ditch their drum machine and recruit a flesh-and-blood drummer. As their music veered away from its industrial leanings and delved deeper into the domain of punk and hard rock, a real man behind the skins seemed a necessity; by Manson's own reckoning, the RX8 had gone over "pretty strangely" in the metal clubs anyway. Fred Streithorst Jr. was tapped for the gig. Fred's new identity was Sara Lee Lucas, unholy spawn of the baked goods magnate Sara Lee and Henry Lee Lucas, the man who eventually inspired the flick *Henry: Portrait of a Serial Killer.*

Henry Lee Lucas was born in 1936 in a two-room cabin in Blacksburg, Virginia, the son of a legless father (the result of a freight train mishap) and a part-time prostitute named Viola. Henry's mother despised her husband and her son, subjecting them to frequent sex shows with the various strangers she'd drag home into her bed. Henry's dad was made so distraught by one such episode that he dragged his body out into the cold, preferring to sleep in the snow, which ultimately led to a fatal case of pneumonia. His mother, now with Henry as her only target, began curling his hair in ringlets and sending him to school dressed as a girl (much like Charles Manson's sadistic uncle). Viola would kill stray animals he brought home as pets. After cutting his eye, she refused to let him see a doctor until it was so infected that it had to be replaced with a glass one. Despite the death of his father, Henry did not want for male guidance for long. His mother's boyfriend, Bernie, introduced Henry to the joys of bestiality, teaching his young charge to rape and torture animals, then finish them off. Soon he graduated to human beings, and at the tender age of fifteen he picked up a local girl, and then strangled her when she told him to back off. He buried her corpse, leaving her murder unsolved for thirty years until he confessed in 1983.

In and out of jail for burglary, Henry finally gained freedom in 1959. After a drunken argument with his charming mom, Henry stabbed her to death. When he was arrested five days later he confessed and bragged of raping the seventy-four-year-old's corpse. He was sentenced to twenty to forty years, but was transferred to a psychiatric hospital for the criminally insane until he was paroled in 1970. After a couple of accusations of child molestation Henry hooked up with twenty-nine-year-old Otis Toole. The two began a prolific killing spree, traveling, raping, and sometimes even devouring their victims (although Lucas claims only Toole ate human flesh). Lucas moved in with Toole's family in 1978 and quickly became infatuated with Otis's ten-year-old niece, Becky. Along with her brother Frank, the four went on the road, where the kids witnessed crimes so horrific that they led to Frank being institutionalized in 1983. Becky and Henry fled to California, where their infatuation soured, and when the girl foolishly slapped Henry, he murdered her and dismembered her corpse. Eventually jailed on a gun-possession charge, Lucas began what would seem an almost endless series of confessions, in excess of five hundred total (although the authorities suspect the truth is closer to one hundred). Later Lucas attempted to recant his confessions, even after he'd led police to bodies. While the complete truth may never be known, authorities are convinced he's responsible for at least one hundred murders.

Marilyn Manson played their first show as a quintet on July 19, 1990. Sara Lee Lucas's membership was announced in a fan newsletter entitled "The Family Trip to Mortville" ("where junkies, queers and killers live scot free!"). But according to the photocopied flyer, the baked goods/percussionist wasn't the only new addition. Lucas's modest photo was laid out beside one of serial killer Jeffrey Dahmer (credited on "chocolate, power saw dismemberment") and Paul Reubens, aka Pee Wee Herman ("kids stuff, auto-erotic asphyxiation"), the eccentric comedian arrested in a Florida adult theater on charges that he'd been openly masturbating during a pornographic movie. The flyer was adorned with Manson's own dark but funny cartoon caricatures of the entire band (including their "new" members), as well as doctored images of the cast of *Scooby Doo* and Dr. Seuss characters, hypodermic needles, handguns, knives, pentagrams, and even David Berkowitz's "Son of Sam" monogram.

The Spooky Kids' distinct visual aesthetic was just one more way in which the group distinguished themselves from their peers. With their evil grins and sunken eyes, Manson's original sketches captured the band's special blend of the silly and the sick, making the band's flyers collectibles long before they seemed destined for stardom. One especially funny handout was a parody of a diner menu, with butcher's cuts of meat on the cover, and the bill of fare listed inside. Salads included "sweet and sour heart prepared in hate sauce" or "candied guts sauted [*sic*] in a creamy filth sauce." Dinner offerings ranged from "one large eye simmered slowly in a fine aqueous humor and glazed in deceit" to "peanut butter and jelly sandwich, sans crust, prepared in a steel carrying case." And for dessert? "A haberdashery of fine rabbit treats, including stew, carrot pot pie, and Charles Nelson Riley [*sic*] pudding."

Manson also designed the original black-and-white eyes logo: the dripping moniker Marilyn Manson sandwiched between Marilyn Monroe's sultry peepers on top, and Charles Manson's menacing glare beneath. The band made sure to start doing promo items besides the tapes and flyers, such as T-shirts and stickers, generating additional visibility, which helped heighten their local profile. They distributed phony Marilyn Manson Family Jive Dollars fashioned from children's play money. And Manson made the most of his connections with the local media, getting the band's name into circulation, even managing to scrounge up airplay for tracks from *big black bus* on local radio stations. The band also began maintaining the "Marilyn Manson Family Intervention Hotline," an information line hooked up to an answering machine.

In January of 1991, the band released yet another four-song tape, *After School Special*. The new titles were "Negative 3," "Lunchbox," "Choklit Factory," and "Cyclops." Among the lyrics for "Choklit Factory" was yet another nod to a serial killer, this time Jeffery Dahmer, who had been employed by a chocolate manufacturer: "Jeff saved for later / His prizes of iniquity / Polaroids to covet / and bones to hide in 213." The liner notes/lyric sheets were designed to mimic school compositions, written on spiral notebook paper, with the comment "too much profanity!" jotted over the words to "Lunchbox."

Just to confuse matters, the next quartet on cassette ("produced and mixed by Daisy B.") was named *Lunchbox*, even though that song didn't appear on it. Instead, the new tunes were "Dune Buggy," "My Monkey," "Learning to Swim," and "Cake and Sodomy." "My Monkey" (which came from the same round of sessions in Miami that produced *Big Black Bus*) featured an opening verse borrowed from an original song by Charles Manson, "Mechanical Man."

As for the inspiration for "Cake and Sodomy," Manson told Florida journalist Mario Tarradell it came from watching cable access television in New York City late at night. "They will show anything," he revealed. "The 976 number ads are real explicit there." But tantalizing sex acts weren't the only thing he was watching. "On the next channel I see some guy talking about God and he's asking for money. It's almost like one God is pornography and the other God is Jesus."

The lyrics to "Learning to Swim," however, came from a different place entirely. "I'm too young to live this life," went the chorus, while the verses featured images like "I grab a sharp stick / and I cut my gills / the water rushes in." What he was alluding to was that, slowly but surely, Marilyn Manson and the Spooky Kids were accumulating a dedicated fan base, and reaching a wider audience. "Over the past year I've had a lot of trouble being in this position I've put myself in, I have the responsibility of influencing the minds of teenagers," he confessed in the same interview with Tarradell. "So I do choose my words . . . because I care. I care about what I say. But you're not going to catch me on MTV commercials saying 'Don't do drugs.' "

Manson definitely had his eye on bigger things, even if his rhetoric hadn't evolved to the level of sophistication fans would come to expect. "I want lunch boxes and dolls," he concluded. "I don't want to change our style to be accepted by the public, I want the public to change their style. I would have no problem if we became the KISS of the '90s."

Soon the band made their premiere appearance on a compact disc. *Funnel Zone*, released in 1991 on the German label Dossier, was compiled by Sync Studios alumni Ralph Cavallaro and Frank "Rat Bastard" Falestra. Among the seventeen cuts by eleven bands were two new tracks by Marilyn Manson, "White Knuckles" and "Strange Same Dogma." With a limited run of five thousand CDs aimed at European metal fans, it's estimated that only a few hundred discs (at best) made the journey across the Atlantic to American shores.

Another important milestone for the band arrived shortly after the New Year. The "Miami Rocks" East Coast Music Forum was held at the Button South club from January 30 through February 2, 1992. With so much music going on in the region, this was an attempt by local promoters, managers, and their cronies to showcase Florida talent on a national level. Local radio and studio people selected bands for showcase slots based on tape submissions from managers, and Marilyn Manson made the cut, landing a show on February 1. (The group's management—John Tovar and Frank Callari—also submitted a song by their charges in Amboog-A-Lard, who were summarily rejected.) A song by the Spooky Kids also wound up on a special "Miami Rocks" promotional compilation, distributed to A and R representatives from various labels.

The band had an official opportunity to gauge their popularity that summer, when the first South Florida Slammie Awards were presented. "Saluting the area's thrash, hardcore and hard alternative bands," the Slammies were conceived as a way to honor these genres, which despite their local prevalence were largely pooh-poohed on a national level. Jim Hayward, a Palm Beach County concert promoter and underground music diehard, organized the awards show and concert (held on June 25 at the Button South) to prove to critics that the South Florida sound was worthy of attention, and possibly even respect. Thanks to a growing, highly vocal fan base, Marilyn Manson were nominated for Best Hard Alternative Band and Band of the Year, putting them up against other regional faves like Malevolent Creation and Raped Ape. The aforementioned Amboog-A-Lard received eight nominations in fourteen categories, and walked away from the evening with five victories, including one for Best Rhythm Guitarist, presented to member Jeordie White. Marilyn Manson and the Spooky Kids left empty-handed.

Meanwhile, the band forged on with their latest cassette-only release, *The Family Jams*. Once again, the title was an allusion to the original Manson: Family Jams was the name of a rock band composed of Manson followers that Charles had attempted to organize and manage. The six fresh tracks were divided up between the two halves of the tape. The one labeled "Side Ma" featured "Dope Hat," "Strange Same Dogma," and "Let Your Ego Die," while the flip "Side Pa" included "Thingmaker," "White Knuckles," and the Beatles pastiche

"Luci in the Sky with Demons." The group's business acumen was clearly increasing, too, for this was the first of the tapes to bear a copyright registration, "© 1992 Berkowitz/Manson." According to the liner notes, all lyrics were provided courtesy of "Mr. Manson," while musical responsibilities lay at the feet of Daisy and Gidget, with additional music by Pogo (with the exception of "Dope Hat," credited solely to Manson and Berkowitz). The tapes had been recorded during '91 and '92 on Daisy's trusty Tascam Porta-One four-track recorder, and mixed by Berkowitz with an assist from Kurt Moody (who'd also been acknowledged on *Lunchbox*). In yet another nod to Charles, Marilyn is credited as "Mr. No Name Manson" in the liner notes.

To anyone paying close attention, Marilyn Manson and the Spooky Kids' star was on the rise. Helaine Blum, manager of the Fort Lauderdale venue Squeeze, where the band played frequently, would later admit in reflection that she'd felt that despite their brilliant ideas, they hadn't really connected right off the bat. But by 1992, Mr. Manson's stage charisma really began to bowl her over. "They're really exceptional at self-promotion, the best I've ever seen down here," she explained to the *Sun-Sentinel* newspaper. "The concept gets people's attention, but then their music is what really hooks them. Since they didn't start out as the greatest musicians, I think it challenged them to be great. A lot of their songs, as weird as they may be, have become anthems. Mr. Manson is such an incredible performer, just extraordinarily riveting. Their straightforward shows are just as powerful as the ones with a lot of theatrics."

The audiences the band was pulling were also increasing, and they could demand better and better rates. A contract between their booking agent, Long Distance Entertainment of Cincinnati, and the Button South guaranteed the band seven hundred dollars for a forty-five-minute set scheduled for September 11, 1992. That is, if the Spooky Kids abided by a few provisions: "No sexual acts, no fire, no animal sacrifices, no nudity. These are prohibited by the club." But regardless of whether or not Manson and company behaved, they couldn't always account for the actions of their audience. "Our crowd was seriously diverse and sometimes it caused a conflict,"

Manson later told *Livewire*. "The metalheads thought we were fags, but they still beat the shit out of themselves in the pit. Usually they feel good enough by the end of the show to go out and harass some other little kids and leave us alone."

By the time of that September Button South show, the band would have undergone one essential change. Marilyn Manson and the Spooky Kids gave their last performance under that billing on August 1, 1992. From here on out, the quintet would be known by the abbreviated appellation Marilyn Manson. To minimize confusion between the group as an entity and their lead singer as an individual, Marilyn himself took to being called Mr. Manson (and later simply Manson, and eventually Rev. Manson). It was a small and seemingly sensible move, but one that might be considered portentous by certain parties in the months to come.

THREE

IN EARLY 1993, MARILYN Manson released their last official limited-edition cassette. *Refrigerator* was an eight-cut compilation of some of their best odds and ends, culled from a couple of different sources. Side One reprised four songs that were already available: "Cake and Sodomy," "Suicide Snowman," "My Monkey," and "Lunchbox." Side Two was composed of a quartet of numbers that had been recorded live on radio station WYNF's *Radio Clash* program, and taken from the tape *Live as Hell:* "Thrift," "Filth," "Wrapped in Plastic," and yet another version of "Dope Hat." Around the same time, a tape called *Marilyn Manson and the Spooky Kids Radio Show* also made the rounds featuring all the cuts from Side Two of *Refrigerator*, plus "Misery Machine," "Learning to Swim," and a brief interview with Mr. Manson.

While the liner notes for *Refrigerator* didn't include lyrics (only three of the songs hadn't been available on a well-known tape before), they did include a lengthy diatribe from Mr. Manson that revealed his congealing aesthetic and preparation to confront the concerns of larger audiences. "I have never pretended to be anything but an asshole. I am what you make me. I'm everything you hate and all you think of being. I am nothing but your fear." He concludes by branding "Christian America" as "the biggest Satan of all." While all the songs were once again copyright Manson and Berkowitz, song credits showed that Gacy and Gein were also contributing to the songwriting process. (Among the acknowledgments to their hairdresser and tattoo artist, the band plugged the merchandise available from Satan's Bakesale, with a staff of three including a young woman named Jessicka.) A total of only one hundred signed, numbered copies—once again with original packaging by Mr. Manson, fashioned to resemble a refrigerator door that opened when the cassette case was lifted—were manufactured and distributed.

In the years that followed, original copies (and even multigenerational duplicates) of all the early Marilyn Manson cassettes became highly sought after by fans. Other songs and spoken word pieces apparently from the same period of 1989 to 1993 also pop up from time to time on bootlegs. Some of them may have appeared on *Snuffy's VCR* or *big black bus*, but for the most part their origins are shrouded in mystery. They include: a reinterpretation of Black Sabbath's "Iron Man" called "Son of Man," "Junk the Magic Dragon," "IV-TV," "Talk of One, Thought of None," "Devil in My Lunchbox," "Number 9," "Cat in the Hat," and a cover of Madonna's controversial "Justify My Love." Manson has also claimed in at least one interview that he was involved in two brief-lived side projects during these years, Mrs. Scabtree (who only performed twice) and Satan on Fire ("a Christian death metal band"): Jessicka of Jack Off Jill supports the former claim.

In May, it was announced that Marilyn Manson had landed a major-label recording contract. The quintet was the first band to sign with Nothing Records, the vanity label started by Trent Reznor of Nine Inch Nails in conjunction with Interscope Records (eventually the roster would swell to include similarly inclined acts like Coil, Pop Will Eat Itself, Pig, Meat Beat Manifesto, and Plug). Mr. Manson and Reznor had maintained contact since their initial encounters. "We just became friends through the fact that we both grew up in Ohio." Manson told *PM* magazine in 1995. "For whatever reason, we had a lot in common. Over the years he and I just kept in touch and turned each other on to what we were working on, talked about music and stuff like that." Trent had already been involved in a protracted legal imbroglio with his original label, TVT Records, for whom he'd recorded *Pretty Hate Machine*. Now that he was more or less master of his own destiny, Reznor wanted his label to be a haven for confrontational artists where their aesthetic wouldn't be interfered with.

"The whole crux of Nothing is that we don't do things like that: we offer complete artistic freedom." Reznor told Matt Ashare in *CMJ New Music Monthly* in 1997. "My experiences with my former record label taught me that you shouldn't fuck with people's art. So I will never fuck with you as an artist. Just know that what you do has repercussions, understand that, and I'll fully support you. Do I support all of Manson's beliefs? No. Do I agree with most of them? No. Would I do that as an artist myself? No, I wouldn't do that personally and I don't have a problem with Interscope not liking it or not wanting to put it out." But he wasn't about to dick around the artists he signed, and tell them they couldn't do things the way they elected to.

To be certain, Marilyn Manson hadn't landed their contract exclusively through the friendship between band members. Other labels, most notably Madonna's own Warner Brothers imprint Maverick, had expressed interest in the group, but always with reservations. Although some found their lyrics to be abrasive to the point of detriment, nobody suggested the band clean up their act or material. Well, not blatantly . . .

"Before we signed with Interscope, Madonna's label was interested in signing us," Manson related to the audience at a 1994 New Music Seminar panel on racism in the music industry. "And her manager called my manager, and said, 'I noticed that the singer has a lot of tattoos. He doesn't have any swastikas on him?' He said, 'No, of course not, one of the guys in the band in Jewish.' 'Oh, okay. We don't have a problem with the Satanism, but we can't deal with any kind of Nazism.' "

There were simply too many hot-button topics wrapped up in the Manson mythos to make them a viable option for most companies. "The bottom line was fear of what we were about," Manson told

Seconds. He claimed that two or three substantial labels had been courting them, "and they all liked the music but didn't like the bags that came along with it. We wanted to have music that was listenable, that people would be able to enjoy, but have a more powerful statement than anything else you'll hear on the radio. And if that kept us off the radio, fine, that was good too." Not what A and R men looking for the next big hit wanted to hear. Even when Marilyn Manson did ink their contract with Nothing, there was some question as to whether they would also officially shake hands with Interscope, the larger label which Nothing went through. But in the end, they did.

Inevitably, signing to a major label inspired some losers to cry foul and damn the band for not aiming lower to maintain underground viability. Manson let loose a healthy dose of venom on the topic soon after in punk zine *Flipside*. "I think it's important that all of the 'pseudo punk rock' kids that are here nowadays realize that punk rock was always about selling out. Don't fucking kid yourself."

"Name every great band, like the Clash, Ramones, Blondie, Sex Pistols, Fear, Germs, X, they've been on a label," Madonna Wayne Gacy added.

"I think you should judge a band on whether they are worthy, regardless of how many people like them," concluded Manson. "The kids just get trapped in this 'indy' [*sic*] mentality where they don't like a band unless nobody else does. They have to be the only ones that have heard about them. I just want them to realize they're cheating themselves."

IF THE BAND HAD any doubts about their ability to cross over on a national level, the nominations for the 1993 South Florida Slammies undoubtedly proved especially encouraging to them. Marilyn Manson was nominated for Band of the Year, Best Hard Alternative Band, Best Local Release (for the *Family Jams* tape), Song of the Year ("Dope Hat"), and Best Vocalist. At the ceremony and show held on July 15 at the Plus Five Club, they snagged two awards, for Best Song and—most importantly—the prestigious Band of the Year. Mr.

Manson was also a presenter, doling out the award for Best National Release to Saigon Kick for their Atlantic Records album *The Lizard*. Saigon Kick (who hadn't even sent a representative) were considered by the majority of scenesters to have abandoned their South Florida roots in pursuit of greener pastures. They were loudly booed down by the disgruntled crowd. Then, according to the post-awards Slammie press release, "presenter Marilyn Manson tossed the award skull into the crowd, where it was smashed in the over-enthusiastic mosh pit."

Mr. Manson hadn't acted alone in this act of mischief. 1992 Slammie Award–winning rhythm guitarist Jeordie White of Amboog-A-Lard (who'd received a paltry two nominations that year) served as his sidekick. But to anyone who knew Manson, that wasn't unusual, as the two were fast friends, despite any rivalry between their bands. Jeordie had been one of the first people Brian Warner met after moving to Florida. Manson recalled their first encounter for *Guitar World*: "I went into a record store to buy Judas Priest's *Turbo Lover*, and I asked him what section it was in. And he was wearing a Bauhaus T-shirt and he had a giant afro. And that's when we first met. And we experienced a love for eighties metal." Among their favorites were Mötley Crüe, Iron Maiden, and Twisted Sister.

From then on, the pair were frequent partners in crime. They'd hang out at the mall, lurking by the pay phones. "They have these little carts in the malls where these girls sell jewelry—earrings and stuff. And we would call up this one girl who was selling those photo T-shirts. We kept making death threats against her until she left the mall in tears. That's when we first started to get along together—in an act of maliciousness at the mall."

Jeordie's own childhood was a bit of a mystery, although he claims it was a far sight more unusual than Brian Warner's. He had been brought up for most of his life by his mother, who the guitarist insists worked as a go-go dancer (in a cage) for Mountain, a New York power rock group fronted by Leslie West who racked up three top 40 albums between 1970 and 1972. "And she used to do the Jerk onstage with the Kinks," he swore to *Guitar World*. "So my dad is probably either Leslie West or Ray Davies. Who knows which one."

(His affable Mom purportedly denies all these tales.) It seems more likely the identity of his father was less fabulous, since he later told *Rolling Stone* his father had gone crazy following a car accident, and abandoned the homestead when Jeordie was six. He also claimed his aunt had been friendly with the Ramones, and dated one of the Bee Gees for a spell.

THE BAND SET OFF to Criteria Studios in Miami to begin recording their debut album. Since Trent Reznor was busy finishing work on his own album, *The Downward Spiral*, Roli Mossiman was tapped to handle production chores. Mossiman boasted an impressive résumé, including membership in revered downtown New York noise terrorists the Swans, production stints with the likes of Machines of Loving Grace and Switzerland's the Young Gods, and a brutal collaborative project with Jim "Foetus" Thirlwell, Wiseblood. A more ideal candidate for capturing the dense, dark, and bracing sound of Marilyn Manson would be hard to locate.

But when the first round of recordings was completed, the outcome proved very different from what the band had anticipated. "It was very slick and it didn't have the raw edge," Manson told writer Michael Workman of Mossiman's vision of the music. "It didn't have all the little sprinkles that we put on all our songs. He kind of smoothed it out and made it more commercial, for whatever reason, which was strange because he's more of an underground producer." When Manson played the tapes for Reznor, he concurred with the thumbs-down verdict. Something had to be done.

But according to Daisy Berkowitz, who'd written the bulk of the musical material being recorded, the sessions at Criteria "went along pretty good.

"I was excited to be in on it," he observes of the recording process. "But there were little instances here and there that kind of bugged me. Like I would get my guitar sound up, and [Manson] would comment on it, or say I was taking the hard way and I should make it easier on myself, that I should change a certain sound or the way

I played something. That would piss me off, because he's not even a musician. It's my guitar playing, my sound.

"Roli Mossiman was kind of in the middle of it. I don't mean 'in the middle' like responsible, I mean just kind of an objective [party]. He didn't have too much to do with changing our sound. But at times, away from Roli, Brian would say to the band, 'I'm the one telling Roli what to do. He just pushes the buttons.' And Roli had a lot of experience. Whether he added to or took away from our sound, I can't really say. Because we recorded the whole record at Criteria, and then Trent said, 'Wow . . . it sounds like a really good demo.' "

Reznor decided that the solution was to dismiss Mossiman, remix the tracks that could be salvaged, and rerecord the remainder. With Trent at the helm, assisted by Alan Moulder and Sean Beavan, the band set off for Los Angeles, and embarked on a seven-week stint in the studio. And this time, there was definitely a clear-cut agenda at play.

"It's a funny thing," recalls Daisy. "When Trent said he wanted to redo the record, Brian flew out to L.A. early, and he was the only one in the band that was out there. So the remixes that they did, I had no say in." Naturally, this did not sit well with the guitarist. When the rest of the band was flown out to commence rerecording at the Record Plant in L.A., they heard the new versions for the first time. And Daisy's opinion was not high on their list of worries. "We got into the studio, and they played us the remixes, and they didn't seem really concerned as to what I thought."

Two years later, when Marilyn Manson were opening for Danzig on the road, Reznor commented to Berkowitz that he'd been very disappointed that the guitarist had seemed so nonplussed upon hearing the new renditions. "I felt like, 'Okay, you remixed 'em, you didn't even call me or anything.' And I felt really excluded. Here they were, just playing me the remixes. I knew that they would not change anything based on me saying, 'Well, I know this should be redone and . . .' It would have been a lot more work to change something that I thought needed to be changed, so I didn't say anything.

"I was glad they were done, but don't throw me a bone," he

grumbles, his voice souring. "I'm in the band, I wrote most of the material, don't throw me a bone."

Adding further to the band's morbid mystique, some of the new recording took shape in Trent's California abode, nicknamed "Le Pig." But Reznor's house was already famous before he'd moved in; it was the exact same dwelling where the real Manson Family had murdered Sharon Tate and several other victims in 1969. Trent had rented the house in 1992. Now he was fulfilling another one of Manson's fantasies. "He had known one of my early dreams or desires was to record at the Sharon Tate house, which I originally wanted to do five years ago when we started the band," confessed Mr. Manson. Much to his chagrin, most of the evidence suggested the house didn't resonate with echoes of the supernatural. "If you thought about what happened there, it was disturbing late at night, but it wasn't exactly a haunted house," Manson told the *Sun-Sentinel*. "No rattling chains or anything, but it did bring across some darkness on the record."

The only truly bizarre episode occurred late one evening. The band was recording "Wrapped in Plastic," which features a line in the chorus "come into our home won't you stay?" The group was working with two twenty-four track machines, running in synch. And for some inexplicable reason, a snippet from "My Monkey" (the song that interpolates a verse from Charles Manson's "Mechanical Man") kept popping up in "Wrapped in Plastic." It was a sample of Charles himself saying, "Why are the kids doin' what they're doin', why did the child reach out and kill his mom and dad?" The whole team decided to call it a night. When they resumed work the next day, the tapes had returned to normal.

The remainder of the task was tackled at the Record Plant. With Trent and his team behind the console, Manson seemed much happier with the results. "Trent and I said we know what this is supposed to sound like," Manson told the *New Times*. "This was our band's first experience in a real studio on a project this big. We didn't know what to expect. It was fifteen-hour days, with a team—Trent, Alan Moulder, Sean Beavan, and me—bringing out the sound."

Not that the boys were all work and no play. Even if they were seasoned professionals, the Record Plant staff apparently didn't take to kindly to some of Manson's more eccentric diversions. He claimed in *Seconds* that transsexual prostitutes worked the corner that the studio was located on, and provided excellent alleviation to longer stretches of tedium. "We started bringing some weird people back to the studio and one of the members in our band had a sexual experience with a transsexual prostitute where he jacked off on its breasts for all of our enjoyment." In exchange for being granted this liberty, they shelled out $150 . . . "The thing that really pissed them off was that she kept coming back the rest of the time we were there," added Madonna Wayne Gacy.

"The rerecording went well," Daisy confirms. "It was the same situation as at Criteria. I felt like everything was pretty cool." Still, there were moments when he wasn't pleased with the direction a track was heading in. "And then it was actually tougher. Because there's Trent and Brian, and Alan Moulder, and Sean Beavan, Trent's engineer." The support network meant protests were futile. "If Trent didn't want to do something, it wouldn't get done. He was surrounded by people who wouldn't disagree with him."

Regardless, Manson and Reznor were pleased with the final results. "He brought out Marilyn Manson," gushed the singer to *Rag* a few months later. Reznor had successfully captured the band's live energy, plus taken advantage of their studio potential, without making them sound like Nine Inch Nails Jr. "He was worried going into it that he was gonna change us too much. But he really brought out what we're about. He brought out the guitar playing and the little things that make us who we are."

But the album's completion wasn't wholly devoid of casualties. By Christmas, Gidget Gein was out of the band. "He felt that his drug addiction was more important than playing bass for us," Mr. Manson quipped, regarding their parting of ways. "We fired our other bass player for being a heroin addict, not for being a heroin addict but for letting heroin use rule his life," he told *Seconds*, after confirming that Florida's drug scene was constantly growing. "We're very much into being strong and having control over our lives because we want to do something, however idealistic it may sound. We don't have time to baby-sit weak people. I tend not to advocate drugs to anybody. Use them how you want. It's your own discretion. We all use drugs in our own ways."

Brad's drug use and erratic behavior had been causing the band increasing numbers of delays and distractions. The band had finally lost patience with his trespasses. "Things like showing up late, showing up for shows really high, and playing really badly, and falling all over the place. I got really tired of it all." The decision to boot him out was unanimous. "We gave him a last chance . . . and a second last chance . . . and I hate doing that. Second and third last chances. Cut to the chase!" But Gidget's ejection from the fold clearly wasn't a malicious act. "Brian wanted to keep Brad in as long as possible, because he was his little court jester. Brad leaving was just basically about his abusing drugs and being irresponsible."

The choice to fill Gidget's pumps seemed inevitable to anyone close to the band. Jeordie White left Amboog-A-Lard, who'd released their first and only album, the nine-track *A New Hope* (on Ty Fy Records), earlier that year. The guitarist, who'd now be switching permanently to bass, also felt joining Marilyn Manson had been kismet. "The day I met him, I knew that we would work together," he told *Rolling Stone*. "As the band gained popularity locally, I thought it was my place to either be in the band, or destroy it."

The new bassist was already a known commodity to Daisy. "Jeordie was in Amboog-A-Lard, and I wasn't into their sound at all. I didn't care for them much." But he also had a very different relationship with Mr. Manson than their guitarist enjoyed. "He hung out with Brian a lot. I didn't. I knew Jeordie was a joker that Brian hung out with." But he wasn't surprised by the initiation of Jeordie into the fold. "I knew early on, if Brad ever OD'd or anything, he would probably replace him." And that wasn't a problem. "All I cared about was if he could play. And he could. And he wasn't on drugs or anything."

And no matter what conflicts might lie ahead, the transition when smoothly. "It was fine," claims Daisy. "He didn't seem to have the attitude that I later realized he had. Which was that of the kid in school that would cut ahead in front of everybody on the lunch line, and get away with it . . . because he knew the bully or something."

The first half of Jeordie's new name surely seemed harmless enough. Twiggy, in honor of the internationally renowned British modeling sensation of the swinging sixties (who'd since moved on to an acting career). For a last name, they turned to Richard Ramirez, better known as the "Night Stalker." By the time he'd been arrested in 1985, Ramirez faced a total of sixty-eight felony counts, including fourteen for murder and twenty-two for rape. His modus operandi was to gain entrance into a home via an open window, and then beat, rape, rob, and sometimes torture or kill his victim. His penchant for drawing satanic pentagrams on his victims' bodies made him all the more frightening. After he was identified and his mug shots were broadcast on TV, he was captured by a mob in East L.A. as he tried to steal a car, but was rescued by the police.

A longtime fan of Satan and Australian heavy metal legends AC/DC, Richard Ramirez infuriated the public by shouting "Hail Satan," and drawing a pentagram on his palm and cheerily waving at cameras during a pretrial appearance. He wanted to plead guilty, but his attorneys talked him into going to trial. He was eventually convicted of thirteen murders and thirty felonies in 1989. Mysteriously, despite his rotting teeth and penchant for rape and murder, Ramirez attracted many female admirers, one of whom eventually married Ramirez in a jailhouse ceremony that most certainly would've defied Martha Stewart's imagination.

"I liked Richard Ramirez because he was into heavy metal," Twiggy told *Guitar World*. "And I chose Twiggy because she was androgynous. She liked to dress like a little boy."

THE FINISHED ALBUM, *PORTRAIT of an American Family*, was handed in to Interscope in January of 1994. And almost immediately there was a flurry of concerns.

First off, there was some skepticism about the name Marilyn Manson. Axl Rose of Guns N'Roses had been in the press a lot at the time, having stirred up quite a brouhaha when word leaked that his band was recording a Charles Manson song for inclusion on their 1993 album of covers, *The Spaghetti Incident?* Yet Mr. Manson confessed that even though he'd hung out with Rose backstage at a show in California during the recording of *POAAF*, the metal guru hadn't shared this tidbit of information. "He was telling me about *The Spaghetti Incident?* record and hadn't mentioned anything about Manson." This displeased Mr. Manson. "I think it's a case of someone with no respect anymore trying to get some notoriety from the underground crowd. I think it was a shallow thing. It was even more shallow that he didn't back himself up on it. He cried to the press like a pussy. It was a publicity stunt that totally backfired," he laughed to *Seconds.*

Even as the heat about the band's name subsided, another spanner was thrown into the works. As the CDs were off being pressed, the quality control executives at Time Warner (who owned a 50 percent interest in Interscope) announced they refused to allow two photographs to appear on the album art. One was what Manson referred to as "my shrine to an ex-girlfriend. There were these bloody Polaroids of a mutilated girl." The concern was that somehow the pictures were linked to a violent crime, and that running them would open the various parties up to a lawsuit.

But funnier still was the concern surrounding the second, a discreet nude shot of a six-year-old Brian Warner . . . taken by his mother. She'd been tickled by the snaps of hirsute Hollywood hunk Burt Reynolds in the buff that had graced the premiere issue of *Cosmopolitan.* "My mom thought it'd be funny to have me do that pose, lying on a couch.

"The point of putting that in there was knowing that people would react and they would be offended and say 'look at this child pornography.' " He told writer Michael Workman. "But it's not and for you to see it as child pornography proves that there's something in your mind that it's not me that's being sick, it's you that's making it sick."

In the end, Manson tried to respect the exorcisms as a necessary evil. "I really wanted those photos in there, it meant something to me." But he also respected that he had to work within the confines of the law. "This is part of me finding out what my boundaries are so I can work to keep pushing the boundaries until they get bigger and bigger. There's twenty states that wouldn't carry it. What's the point in having something cool if no one can buy it?"

Faced with so many complaints, Manson's management, the TCA Group, began courting new suitors should they part ways with Interscope. Once again, Maverick expressed interest. But this time the Material Girl herself voiced a complaint: She didn't approve of Pogo's name (even though she'd also adopted it as part of reinventing her own persona in the first place). "I explained to her that it was a compliment but she didn't quite get it," chuckled Manson in *Film Threat*. But at the eleventh hour, Interscope granted them a reprieve, and two days before the scheduled release date, Interscope announced they would stick with the band.

The new lineup had been rehearsing for months, in preparation for their first official tour, opening for NiN on their Self-Destruct tour. They began with a handful of club dates in Chicago, Dallas, Boston, and New York, doing their first big round of press along the way. Even though their album release was still two months away, the packed house of NiN fans was sufficiently blown away by Manson's unbridled fury on stage at the Webster Hall date on May 13. (They were less pleased when, after Reznor's set, the authorities blocked all but one exit, severely curtailing the flow of traffic out of the venue.) In an especially odd twist of booking, the next night NiN and Manson shared the bill at Roseland with faux lesbian dance act Fem2Fem.

In between the New York shows and the band's next big dates in Atlanta at the end of July, Manson took some time out to produce tracks with local girl band Jack Off Jill. Conveniently, JOJ front person Jessicka (née Jessica Fordera) was not only roommates with Melissa, Manson's current girlfriend, but had been dating Twiggy. "They sounded like the Go-Go's, before the Go-Go's went commercial . . . only nastier," says an insider that visited the studio during the sessions. Eventually Manson would be credited for producing and mixing the Jack Off Jill tune "Don't Wake the Baby," which appeared on the *South Florida Slammie Awards Vol. 1* CD (GJ Records, 1994). He also coproduced and mixed both sides of their single "My Cat Can Eat a Whole Watermelon" b/w "Swollen" (Rectum Records, 1994).

On June 9, the nation got its first official taste of Marilyn Manson, with the release of the single and video for "Get Your Gunn." The sleeve for the disc featured a picture of a young child, Twiggy's half brother Wes Brown. A video for the cut was also shot, and accepted by MTV, but almost never aired, although it did pop up on *Headbangers' Ball*. In the *New Times*, Manson claimed there was a "big hassle" over the lyrics, specifically the chorus "goddamn/oh Lord/ goddamn," even in the radio edit. "They wanted they word *God* bleeped, which is assbackward because *damn* is the cussword."

"What's great is that this is the most uncommercial track, the most politically incorrect," Manson told the *Sun-Sentinel*. The song had originally been inspired by the tragedy of Dr. David Gunn. On March 10, 1993, after enduring years of harassment, threats, and clinic blockades, the Pensacola, Florida, physician—who performed legal abortions—was murdered by a right-wing activist. The previous summer, Wanted posters targeting the doctor and containing his photograph, home address, telephone number, and daily schedule had been distributed at a rally sponsored by Operation Rescue in Montgomery, Alabama. Naturally, the reaction of some antichoice leaders to Dr. Gunn's slaying in 1993 had reiterated the extremism displayed by some pro-lifers. One member of the American Family Association was quoted as saying, "I think the man that was killed . . . should be glad he was not killed the same way that he has killed other people, which is limb by limb."

The title of the non-LP track "Revelation #9" was a sarcastic nod to the influence of the Beatles and their experimental "Revolution No. 9," which featured a classic example of "phonetic reversal," one of several techniques for backward masking. On the Fab Four cut, a voice with a British accent repeats "Number nine, number nine . . ." ad nauseam. When the phrase is deconstructed in reverse, it sounds something akin to "turn me on dead man." Some of the samples in the Manson collage were from intercepted phone calls, stitched together with lyrics to help tie the track with "Get Your Gunn." But the cut is especially remarkable for Pogo's sonic manipulations, including his own foray into backward masking. He claimed that there were thirteen tracks total running, with at least six of them backward. "It is equally playable in any direction."

To celebrate the pending release of *Portrait of an American Family*, the band hosted a listening party on Wednesday, June 29, at one of their oldest haunts, Fort Lauderdale's Squeeze. Among the guests were assorted N.Y. and L.A. record label executives, as well as the heads of two of Florida's biggest recording studios, Tom Morris of Tampa's Morrissound and Joel Levy of Miami's Criteria. The band performed "a rare acoustic set" including two covers: "Sweet Dreams (Are Made of This)" by the Eurythmics and "I Put a Spell on You" by Screamin' Jay Hawkins. Reznor held court at the bar.

While Manson had always taken pains to paint his relationship with Reznor as one of friendship, at least one source close to the band during the period feels both parties were a bit more opportunistic. "Trent and Brian each see things in the other that he wants to be. Brian wants to be as in control of his business affairs as Trent is. Trent wants to be perceived as being as dangerous as Brian is perceived to be. Trent wants to be bad, and for a while, he was bad vicariously through Brian. Brian wants to learn about recording and producing, and watched Trent very carefully."

A few days after the party, on Sunday, July 3, Marilyn Manson headlined the 1994 Slammie Awards, held at the Edge in downtown Fort Lauderdale. Over 1,200 hard-rock fans joined them for the show, which featured five other bands (including Jack Off Jill), culminating with Manson's intense forty-five-minute set. With the release of their official debut still a week away, Marilyn Manson were only nominated in two categories, Band of the Year and Best Vocalist. They had no trouble walking off with both prizes, winning their second Grand Slammie in a row, and Mr. Manson even snagged himself a free tattoo from Slammie sponsor Outrageous Tattoos for the latter achievement.

Through all this, the singer continued to live with his parents in Boca Raton. In a cover story for *XS* timed to coincide with the album's release, Ted Kissell describes Manson's bedroom at the Warner homestead in a restricted-access, gated community. A display of metal lunch boxes included *The Partridge Family, Hee Haw,* KISS, *The Hardy Boys,* and *Wonderbug* specimens. The bookshelf, on which *Planet of the Apes* and *Six Million Dollar Man* action figures cavorted, featured titles like *Satan Wants You* and *Raising Hell: An Encyclopedia of Devil Worship.* A plethora of Manson show flyers, featuring his original drawings and collages, dotted the walls. And, of course, a stereo, and the television via which he'd absorbed so many talk shows. Yet oddly enough, he opted not to disclose his given name to the writer, claiming he'd been the target of harassment in the past. Someone had even gone so far as to leave a severed head from a plaster cow on his doorstep.

But already, the divisions between Brian Warner and Marilyn Manson were beginning to blur beyond distinction. "It's not like I turn off Marilyn Manson and I'm an everyday guy who goes and has another job and doesn't think about any of this stuff," he said to *XS.* "Marilyn Manson is the most real thing that can come from me."

Four

PORTRAIT OF AN AMERICAN *Family* was the aesthetic consummation of Marilyn Manson's four-year gestation. A line from "Dogma," "You cannot sedate all the things you hate," was emblazoned on the disc itself, a declaration of intention. "The music is brutal, the lyrics are shocking, and this is one of the weirdest albums of the year," reckoned the *Sun-Sentinel* in their review. While much of the national press dismissed the band as little more than cartoonish protégés of Reznor, *POAAF* certainly offered plenty of material for fans to sink their teeth into.

The album kicked off with "Prelude (The Family Trip)," a monologue lifted from the film *Willy Wonka and the Chocolate Factory,* as "adapted by Manson," accompanied by a musical bed courtesy of Manson and Pogo. The creepy rant originally appears in what is arguably the movie's most disturbing sequence in a picture that has a phenomenal number of them (especially in light of the fact it was ostensibly made for children). The young prizewinners and their guardians board a small boat piloted by the confectioner Wonka, only to disappear into a dark tunnel. With barely suppressed hysteria, he begins to chant, "There's no earthly way of knowing/ which direction we are going/Not a speck of light is showing. . . ."

"Mary Had a Little Lamb" it's not. Meanwhile, nightmarish visions—a chicken being decapitated, hideous insects and reptiles—and garish lights flash up around the children.

Manson freely admitted to anyone who asked that *Willy Wonka* was his favorite movie. "I myself, just like everyone else, love fear," he said of the scary boat ride. "And I especially like the phenomenon of villains in children's movies, and what makes kids scared of them." Willy Wonka, the Child Snatcher from *Chitty Chitty Bang Bang*, and even Dr. Suess's *Cat in the Hat* all received high marks. And by his accounts, what contemporary tots were being weaned on simply didn't compare. "I watch some stuff today, but stuff today is very watered down," he told *Alternative Press*. "As kids we used to see some really terrifying stuff, but it was really candy-coated so it was given to us more subversively. Now, it's an R-rated movie, and if you're a kid and you get to see it that way, but you don't see it in the G-rated movies. It's a weird way that things have evolved. I'm really into the old stuff. I like to scare little kids. I like little kids, I feel that I still am a little kid, so there's a strange relationship with that."

He elaborated on his specific attraction to the Wonka character later in *RIP*. "I thought Willy Wonka represented the devil, and I've always been attracted to the bad guy. Why was he the bad guy? Later I realized that it's all according to perspective. If you're standing with the bad guy, then somebody else is the bad guy. But I always thought Willy Wonka represented that dark side, because he lured the children with the sweets and things that were forbidden." Like Manson himself, Wonka wasn't afraid to stand apart from the crowd, or tempt children to deviate from accepted behavior patterns. "He even had a bit of morality because the kids who didn't listen to what he was saying were punished and didn't win in the end," he noted in the *Times Reader*. "I've always related to him on that level."

In addition to a plethora of lip service, Mr. Manson also went so far as to include Roald Dahl's *Charlie and the Chocolate Factory* on his "Advised Reading and Listening List" as early as the *Reality Transmission M1* (fall 1994) newsletter. Yet three years later, representatives for Dahl (who wrote the screenplay for *Willy Wonka*) had only reserved opinions on possibly their most controversial advocate. In a letter dated July 23, 1997, Ms. Amanda Conquy of Dahl & Dahl, who administers the Dahl literary estate on behalf of the author's family, shared these opinions: "I am afraid I have no view on the influence that 'Willy Wonka' might have had on Mr. Manson." Conquy admits this is partially because she is unfamiliar with the Manson oeuvre, but also because "Mr. Dahl had very little control or involvement" over the Warner Brother production.

However, in reviewing press materials on the band, she did discern parallels between the two distinctly different artists. "Reading the articles it does seem to me that both Manson and Dahl have an inherent appeal for young people in that they do not flinch from what kids around the world so clearly and intuitively understand— that there is a difference between good and evil. They see it all around them, from the classroom, to the playground and to the wider world. From time immemorial classic children's books and fables have reflected this."

Bellowing "I am the god of fuck," a line lifted from Charles Manson, Marilyn and his cohorts ripped into a powerful new vision of "Cake and Sodomy" next. " 'Cake and Sodomy' was when I first fell into what has become my writing style, whatever that is," he noted in *RIP*. Meanwhile, lyrics like "VCRs and Vaseline/TV fucked by plastic queens/cash in hand and dick on screen/who said God was ever clean?" substantiate Manson's claim that much of the song's inspiration came from watching phone sex ads in New York City.

"Lunchbox" continued the theme of childhood injustices. As Manson pointed out in the band's promotional material, the state of Florida had passed a law in 1972 banning metal lunch boxes. "For fear that heavy boxes could be used as weapons in the hands of children, the metal content was outlawed in several states and Canada."

"I remember I got a KISS lunch box, and I wasn't allowed to bring it to school because they said it was Satanic," reflected Manson in *Alternative Press*. "That really upset me, because I was a big KISS fan around that time. I saved that lunch box, and I still have it. I

THE CHEESE STANDS ALONE.
Manson on his lonesome, circa summer of 1994

(Frank Frenzi/LFI)

An early Manson Family portrait.
Note Twiggy's Bee Gees lunch box! Clockwise from top:
Daisy Berkowitz, Sara Lee Lucas, Twiggy Ramirez,
Marilyn Manson, Madonna Wayne Gacy

(Melanie Weiner)

DAISY BERKOWITZ CHEERFULLY SIGNING
a stack of photos for fans on the Smells Like Children tour

(Brian D. Garrity)

THE BODY IS A MAP.
Manson's torso during the self-mutilation days

(Brian D. Garrity)

GOING BACK TO THEIR ROOTS.
Manson and Twiggy descend on the mall with wide-eyed glee
(Brian D. Garrity)

THE ANTICHRIST LIVE ON STAGE
(Kristin Callahan/LFI)

Manson, Madonna Wayne Gacy,
and Zim Zum at OzzFest '97
(Frank Frenzi/LFI)

Marilyn Manson and Smashing Pumpkins' Billy Corgan
at the 1996 MTV Music Video Awards
(Kevin Mazur/LFI)

started collecting lunch boxes around five years ago. When I found that KISS lunch box it reminded me of that whole era.

"We're a very nostalgic band, we're very into our childhood, because we don't want to let that go. Because childhood is a magical time when kids believe things, and if you believe something it will come true for you. That's the thing, adults they get so depressed, so jaded because everything is so horrible, that they stop believing in dreams and they don't try and live them out. They can't live, because they're so busy trying to make money and pretend to live, but nobody really gets to enjoy themselves."

"Lunchbox" was the musical manifestation of the chip Brian Warner had developed on his shoulder after years of mistreatment at the hands of school bullies and authority figures alike. In *RIP* he likened the sentiments of the song's protagonist "to the mentality of a lot of books I've read on people like Richard Ramirez or Jeffrey Dahmer, in that these people had been fucked with for all their lives and that their only way to lash out and to pay back everyone who had fucked them over was through murder. Obviously I found a different outlet, but I think the mentality and the attitude is real similar."

After "Lunchbox," "Organ Grinder" and "Cyclops" (which popped up in the Oliver Stone motion picture *Natural Born Killers,* for which Reznor coordinated the sound track) provided a segue into another one of *POAAF's* high points, "Dope Hat." "It's about how people are entertained by my ability to balance between addiction and control," he claimed in a Q&A session for *Spin OnLine.* Lines like "My big top tricks will always make you happy/But we all know the hat is wearing me" also suggested that the struggles of Gidget Gein (aka Brad Stewart) had impacted on Manson's feelings about drugs, too. "I thoroughly advocate the use of drugs," he insisted in *Seconds.* "I completely hate the abuse of drugs. I have no problem with people using drugs and doing whatever they like to do but when they start abusing them, that's when there's a problem. I'll never get to that point, because I don't have that kind of personality."

But "Dope Hat" also featured elements alluding to the playful side of Marilyn Manson, emphasizing the central dichotomy of the band once more. Samples of actor Charles Nelson Reilly peppered the track, snippets of utterances from the Great Hoodoo, the evil magician who'd terrorized the Hat People in Sid and Marty Krofft's Saturday morning TV series *Lidsville*. The vividly colored, hallucinatory fantasy world of the Kroffts' shows [*H. R. Pufnstuf, The Bugaloos, Sigmund & the Sea Monsters*] seems to have been an early Manson influence second only to Willy Wonka and Anton LaVey," observes fan Judy Pope.

The inspiration behind "Get Your Gunn" (which would also later spring up on a movie sound track, for *S.F.W.*) had come partially from the senseless murder of Dr. David Gunn. But as Manson revealed years later in *Rolling Stone*, abortion had always been a grim fixation of his. As a youngster, while playing near a butcher's store across the street from his parent's house, he'd come across a coffee can swarmed by flies. "I opened it up, and it had an aborted fetus in it. My parents told me that it was just raw meat." A practical joke, they insisted, but the image was branded into his memory. "That was just the scariest thing ever," he added in *Seconds*, "because I was just looking through shit in the garbage, and you open this can, and there's a little face looking at you and it was really sick."

The topic would continue to manifest itself in his songs. And not just because of the coffee can. "But actually I've had to go through that experience, with a girl," he told *Rolling Stone*. "And it was real bad, too, because it was like four months into her being pregnant, and they had to do some real intense things where they induce labor. Very terrifying stuff."

"Wrapped in Plastic" segued into "Dogma," which (as "Strange Same Dogma") had been one of his earliest compositions with Berkowitz. The latter was one of two songs to feature guest star Hope Nichols, who contributed backing vocals, as well as the saxophone noodling on "Get Your Gunn." The former lead singer of Fetchin' Bones and a veteran of industrial behemoth Pigface (which had also featured Reznor in one incarnation), Nichols had caught Manson's eye fronting Charlotte, North Carolina outfit Sugarsmack. "I think it's very refreshing," she commented of the Manson phenomenon, then cryptically noted, "with whatever's going on inside, I think it's better he's in a rock band."

"Sweet Tooth" was bloated with images of codependency and craving relationships despite knowing their pitfalls. The title itself also hinted at one of Manson's own vices: sugar. "I'm addicted to sugar, I guess," he told writer Leah Lin. "Caramello bars because they are so thick and sugary. They almost make you sick just to eat them." In another interview, with Michael Brighton, he confessed that as a child he'd only consume the flavored marshmallows in Frankenberry cereal, practically copping "the Twinkie defense." "It's real typical how everything now is so conservative and it's fucked up because you grow up being accustomed to those kind of cereals, and now everything is Nutrasweet, low salt, all this bullshit."

"Snake Eyes and Sissies" was followed by "My Monkey," another song that drew literally on the Charles Manson legacy. Young Robert Pierce (aged six at the time) made his recording debut on the track. His father had owned the Marilyn Manson Family's early cassette releases, and played them around young Robert. "The song is very nursery rhyme-ish, and sounds like a children's song." Robert learned the song by rote. Manson was utterly smitten when he heard him, and little Bobby's fate was sealed. "There's points where my voice and the child's voice mutate together and you can't tell who is who," he gushed to *Alternative Press.* "I think that's my favorite part of the record, because it's where I really get to become a child again."

The album's final song, "Misery Machine," contains one of Manson's more arcane lyrical references: "we're gonna ride to the abbey of Thelema." The title is a pun on the name of the van on the cartoon *Scooby-Doo,* one of Manson's favorites. "I was always into Scooby-Doo, I've always had a thing for [the character] Daphne," he confessed to *Black Market.* "I remember my first realization with a hard-on because of Daphne." Since one of the other teen sleuths on the show was named Thelma, could Manson merely have made a bizarre spelling error?

Manson expert Judy Pope claims that's not the case, noting that

"Thelema" translates as "will" in Greek. "The Abbey of Thelema was famed sorcerer Aleister Crowley's temple and proposed academy of the magickal arts in Cefalu, Italy," she writes. "Crowley hoped to establish both a worldwide center of magickal studies and a steady source of income (via tuition fees) for himself with this project, but it failed to attract the attention he hoped, and [dictator Benito] Mussolini's government eventually ejected Crowley from the country." In addition to influence on other rock artists, such as Led Zeppelin, Crowley, who died in 1947, is perhaps best known for his pronouncements "Love is the Law, Love Under Will" and "Do What Thou Wilt shall be the whole of the Law."

The lyrics throughout the album were spartan, lean but strong and fighting mad. They also hinted at his writing background, and (without being highbrow) drew on his love for puns, alliteration, metaphors, and double entendre. "I love reading things like that, and I appreciate when it takes place," he told one interviewer. "I've tried a lot to write in parable forms." He was not only tinkering with real parables from the Bible, but also struggling to see if they were still a legitimate form of communication. "How well does that get across your message?" he mused. "It seems like it works, to a certain degree. So I guess parables are a valuable part of storytelling."

Certainly many distinctive moments on *POAAF* came courtesy of Pogo's samples, ranging from the bits of Child Catcher dialogue appropriated from *Chitty Chitty Bang Bang* to several stellar moments from cult actress Mink Stole in the films of John Waters (the "Go home to your mother" rant at the end of the album comes from *Desperate Living*).

Likewise, the keyboard player continued to fiddle with backward masking, with rumors that such pious ditties as "Onward, Christian Soldiers" were buried deep in the mix of *POAAF*. "Remember, if you get something devil and backmask it, you reverse it and it becomes good," he told the *Gaston Gazette*. Satanic sentiments played backward send good messages, and vice versa. "So if you want to make something evil, you take a Christian thing and play it in reverse. So when you play it forward, which is the way you would normally play a CD, it is reverse so it is the opposite of what it means." Apparently Led Zeppelin hadn't considered this when composing the words to "Stairway to Heaven," which when phonetically reversed, contain no less than six references to Satan and rejecting Christianity. But Pogo and the Manson family had. "So all of our backward messages are about the Lord, and we are very excited about that." Thus Marilyn Manson joined the proud ranks of numerous other artists who've deliberately used various backward masking techniques, including Black Oak Arkansas, ELO, Frank Zappa, Prince, and Pink Floyd.

But perhaps the record's most memorable bit of sonic debris was hidden almost ten minutes after the close of "Misery Machine." Apparently, an enraged parent had taken advantage of the band's Marilyn Manson Family Intervention Hotline phone number to spew some retaliatory venom.

"I want my son off of your mailing list," the anonymous caller demands in clipped tones. "I have already contacted the post office about your pornographic material that is being received in the mail. My next stop is my attorney. I do not want this number called anymore, and I do not want anything delivered to my address. If I receive anything else from this band, or this group, my next phone call will be my attorney, and you will be contacted. Thank you and good-bye!"

FIVE

BEFORE OFFICIALLY HITTING THE road with the full-fledged "Self Destruct" tour, the bands played a few more warm-up dates. For the August 6 gig at the remote Molson Park in Barrie, Ontario, Canada, Reznor imported another recent Nothing signing, UK sample-happy rock act Pop Will Eat Itself. Also on the bill were Seattle foursome Soundgarden. Ironically, while the ethics of "grunge" espoused denouncing the trappings of rock stardom, Soundgarden not only spent the bulk of the afternoon hidden away in their dressing bungalow, but insisted that the yard of the artists' compound—where other performers, industry types, and fans were socializing—be completely cleared when they finally emerged for their show.

On the other hand, Reznor behaved in a surprisingly gracious manner to the fans on the other side of the fenced-in encampment. And although *Portrait of an American Family* had only been out for a month, already a clutch of devotees in striped stockings and garish eye makeup hopped around excitedly, swinging their lunch boxes and hoping for a glimpse of Mr. Manson and company. Meanwhile backstage, Mr. Manson proudly showed off the proof sheets from his recent shoot with notorious underground photographer Richard Kern. Nude (with privates tucked between his legs) against a bright red background, his lipstick smeared all over his face, Manson paid homage to the celebrated *Playboy* spread that had secured the fame of his other namesake, Marilyn Monroe.

On August 29 they settled in for the long haul, getting things off to a rousing start with two dates on Trent's home turf, at the Nautica Stage in Cleveland, Ohio. These were the first of six nights that featured yet another outrageous act: Courtney Love's band Hole. In turmoil since the suicide of her husband Kurt Cobain four months earlier, Love proved just as adept at orchestrating chaos as the other bands on the bill.

"She's just really nuts," Manson told *Gear*. The band shared a dressing room with Hole at the Nautica, which the men of Manson commemorated with candid shots of Love in the raw. "She's in our dressing room trying on all of her clothes, naked, we're snappin' pictures like there's no tomorrow." The first night Mr. Manson typically wound up half-naked and simulating masturbation on stage, while Love ripped off her top during the set. By the second night, the boys were trying to convince her to join them for a number. "We talked her into doing 'Helter Skelter' with us tonight," he announced. "We don't normally do it but we figured that's a song that she'd probably know."

Love's reputation as a party girl ensured that soon rumors were flying that a member of Marilyn Manson may have enjoyed her carnal favors. When Boyd Rice quizzed Twiggy on the subject in *Seconds*, the bassist proved remarkably respectful of La Love, insisting that while she could be "a pain in the ass," and that "she used to beat me up when we were on tour together for my per diems," she could also act as a great friend. "Actually, she's pretty sweet underneath all that. As far as her being famous, it didn't make anything more exciting."

In Muncie, Indiana, the notorious Jim Rose Circus Sideshow joined the tour. Rose's sensationalist troupe of contemporary carnival freaks fit in with the bill perfectly. "America's need for something like Marilyn Manson or Jim Rose is exactly what has created it," Manson told *Generation*. The admiration was mutual all around. "On that teenage night when I lost my virginity, if Marilyn Manson had been played loudly, I would have had a better orgasm," wrote Rose in *RIP*.

On September 24 the freak show rolled into Rose's hometown, Seattle, Washington. Having been smitten with *POAAF* right off the bat, Veronica Kirchoff traveled up from neighboring Tacoma to interview Mr. Manson for her fanzine *Levity*. Although she almost bolted out of sheer nervousness, she managed to tough it out until he emerged from backstage after sound check. "So he comes up and shakes my hand. 'I'm Marilyn.' He was just wearing a black T-shirt, black jeans shorts, very little makeup and huge sunglasses covering his whole face." They went outside to escape the noise. "We're just sitting in the grass, and people are walking by. Nobody knows who these guys are. They're here for Nine Inch Nails, and giving us— these two freaks on the lawn—weird looks." Their chat went smoothly enough, although Manson kept shifting around her. "When we first sat down he was sitting in front of me, over to one side, and the sun was in his face. So he moves over a little bit . . . then moves over here . . . then over here . . . and eventually he ended up almost behind me." When they wrapped up, he invited her to come to the after-show party at Moe's, a local rock club Rose had a financial interest in, and told her to get a VIP pass from the stage manager.

She scoured the crowd before the show, hoping to meet some kindred spirits, but even folks up front wearing the infamous KILL GOD / KILL YOUR MOM AND DAD / KILL YOURSELF T-shirts had just purchased them at the venue because they looked cool. "Nobody had heard of Marilyn Manson," she recalls. But they damn well knew who they were by the end of their short set. "I found a lot of people after the show and asked them, and their jaws were dropping. He stuck a bottle up his ass! Kids don't see that every day. People were just dumbfounded." The reaction wasn't unanimously positive ("A lot of people I asked said, 'Oh, they sucked' "), but the band had definitely made their mark on the Emerald City NiN fans. "It left an impression on me," she says, voicing a sentiment countless other neophytes would soon echo. "Seeing them for the first time was very lasting."

After the show, she chatted with Daisy for a minute and eventually convinced the tour manager to slip her a VIP pass. She made her way backstage, but couldn't find Manson, whom she still needed to photograph for her story. Finally he came round a bend, back in his street clothes again, and told her to pop into the Nine Inch Nails dressing room, where they were unwinding. Even though she'd seen her share of unruly scenes in industrial clubs, she remembers being surprised by the festivities. "They were playing Crisco Twister, and Manson was spraying butane on everything and catching it on fire. He sprayed this guy's leg and set him on fire." Two young female groupies came up to Manson and inquired after the big black phallus he'd whipped out of his pants during their set. "And he's like, 'It's right here,' grabbing a handful of his crotch," she laughs.

Having no transportation of her own, Kirchoff asked Manson to help her get across town to Moe's as the crowd started thinning out backstage. "And he says, 'Hold on, wait here, I'm gonna see if it's okay with Trent if you go with us on his bus.' " A huge NiN fan, the teenager was bowled over a few minutes later, when she stepped into Reznor's coach and Manson introduced them. She played with Trent's dog, laughed as he threw three boxes of substandard pizza out the door into the night, and quietly bemoaned being saddled with hefty anthologies of angst-ridden teen poetry by fans night after night.

When they walked into the club, Reznor was clearly the center of attention. "And Manson is still running around setting everything on fire. He's like spreading garbage on the floor and making little bonfires everywhere. And this big black bouncer comes up to him and tells him, 'You're gonna have to stop doing that.' And Manson swore at him and said 'I'm a member of one of the bands, this party is for me.' " Fortunately, Jim Rose got him off the hook, but Manson decided to lay off on the lighter fluid for a while. Other band members picked up the pyromania where their frontman had left off, until the party wound down at closing time. "When we left, there was an entire stall in the women's bathroom that was on fire." (Eventually Manson chilled out on the firebug action; "I've been on this 10-day

'No fire, no Jack Daniel's' program," he told *Black Market* later in the tour.)

The crowd retired to the sidewalk, and while Veronica was milling about, the NiN bus pulled off. Suddenly she realized that her bag, containing her wallet and house keys, was still on the coach. "All I had were the clothes I was wearing." Recognizing this could pose a serious problem, Manson told her not to worry, and arranged with their tour manager to retrieve it from Trent's hotel . . . in the morning. Kirchoff decided to just roll with the situation, and returned with the band to their motel, half an hour outside town. She went into the room Manson and Twiggy were sharing, where the rest of the band was hanging out. "Pogo was drinking, and Daisy was just standing around. Twiggy was lying on his bed, and throws his legs in the air, and farts." He cried out for a lighter and spent the better part of the next few minutes trying to be a human blowtorch. "Repeatedly! That boy has gas.

"And then Manson just yells, 'Get the hell out!' and they run out and slam the door." Twiggy dozed off, and Veronica concentrated very hard on just watching television. "I was, understandably, a little bit nervous. So I'm sitting on the end of the bed, and Manson says 'you can take off your shoes, you look really uncomfortable.' " She took off her shoes, and then scooted back and reclined against the headboard. They started talking, about everything from body piercing to her family. He inquired repeatedly if she should telephone home. "He was really concerned about that, which I thought was kind of funny." They ended up talking (and that's all!) until six or seven in the morning. "And it was cool. Because when I interviewed him I was getting Marilyn Manson, but when I got to talk to him later, it was Brian."

The rest of the band scurried around all night, tormenting each other "knocking on the doors and pretending to be the cleaning staff." But in the morning, the real housekeeping staff woke them up. The band slowly pulled their act together, and went to breakfast at Denny's around noon, Veronica still in tow. "And he paid for my breakfast," she recalls. "I had just met the guy, he has no obligation, and he totally took care of me." They fetched her bag from Trent's hotel, and dropped her at the bus station. "I got out and gave Manson a hug." He asked for a copy of her interview and promised to keep in touch. She dutifully sent him the story, but didn't get a response. At least, not for a long time . . .

AFTER A VISIT TO Canada, the tour continued down the coast through California. In Sacramento, Manson's antics with the big black phallus managed to make the papers. "Ya wanna see a rock star's cock?!" read the opening sentence of columnist Rudeboy's notice in the *Sacramento News and Review*, who also observed that a lot of NiN fans didn't dig the Manson set, and even booed at points.

They played Los Angeles for the first time on October 3, then again on the sixth and seventh. After one show, former underage porn star turned serious actress Traci Lords materialized backstage and approached Manson. "I don't know for what reason, because if I was her, I would never come up to somebody that looked like me. I had red lipstick all over my face and looked like either a prostitute or an extra from a David Lynch outtake," he confessed to *Seconds*, pronouncing her "one of the coolest people that I've ever met. I respected her for going on with her life after all that she came through. I think she's pretty strong." The two hit it off, and once again rumors flew. Manson would later deny any hanky-panky to the press, but whatever information about the couple leaked back to his then-girlfriend back home, it was enough to break up their relationship (if only temporarily).

But the most important meeting of Manson's swing through California was played out behind closed doors, when he was granted an audience with Dr. Anton Szandor LaVey, founder of the Church of Satan and author of *The Satanic Bible*. Manson had been talking about Satanism in the press for several years, and in the band's fall '94 *Reality Transmission* newsletter included LaVey's *Devil's Notebook* (alongside books by Nietzsche, Roald Dahl, and cult film director John Waters) on his required reading list for Spooky Kids. The band had even approached LaVey about playing theremin on a *POAAF* track. The doctor had contacted Manson and suggested they meet, and when the band swung through San Francisco, they did. Recognizing Manson's increasingly prominent public profile, LaVey appointed Manson a reverend in the Church of Satan.

"LaVey is a huge influence on a lot of the things I do," Manson admitted in *Seconds* shortly after the release of *POAAF*. "I'm not part of any specific religion but that's not a religion anyway, if you're really into it." While many people misconstrue Satanism as worshiping the devil, they're wrong. Worshiping the devil would imply believing in a Christian God, which true Satanists don't.

Although a variety of belief systems have been labeled Satanism over the centuries, and the history of Satanists has often been revised or obscured by their opponents the Christians, there are a few attributes common to virtually all who accept the designation. The average Satanist holds beliefs at odds with the tenets of Christianity, does not adhere to the idea of an absolute moral code, and emphasizes the supremacy of the rights of the individual over those of the greater public. (And as one expert points out, in these regards Satanists have much in common with members of the Libertarian Party.) Followers of LaVey's specific teachings "believe in individualism, gratification of the ego, self-reliance and the ideal of the Nietzschean Superman," "use Magick as a tool for earthly power," and "see Satan as the driving force behind achievement in mankind."

"It's about realizing, much like Nietzsche said, that you are your own god," Manson told Jim Rose in *RIP*. Worship, therefore, should be conducted accordingly. "Life is the Great Indulgence and Death is the Great Abstinence, as there is no afterlife." The basic concepts of *The Satanic Bible* can be found in LaVey's answer to the Bible's Ten Commandments, the Nine Satanic Statements:

1. Satan represents indulgence, instead of abstinence!
2. Satan represents vital existence, instead of spiritual pipe dreams!
3. Satan represents undefiled wisdom, instead of hypocritical self-deceit!
4. Satan represents kindness to those who deserve it, instead of love wasted on ingrates!

5. Satan represents vengeance, instead of turning the other cheek!
6. Satan represents responsibility to the responsible, instead of concern for psychic vampires!
7. Satan represents man as just another animal, sometimes better than, more often worse than those that walk on all fours, who, because of his "divine spiritual and intellectual development," has become the most vicious animal of all!
8. Satan represents all of the so-called sins, as they all lead to physical, mental, or emotional gratification!
9. Satan has been the best friend the church has ever had, as he has kept it in business all these years!

Manson was by no means the first rock star to delve into Satanism. From Led Zeppelin to Glenn Danzig, various rock stars flirted with ideas and philosophies espoused by LaVey and his followers. But in the months and years to come, Manson would evolve into the church's best-known and most articulate spokesperson ever in the realm of showbiz. "We're received a number of inquires from kids who first got interested in Satanism because of Marilyn Manson's music and attitudes," writes Blanche Barton of the Church of Satan on Manson's involvement with the church. "The Doctor feels one reason Mr. Manson's popular is because he's the Real Thing. He makes no secret about his advocacy of true Satanic ideals—and he's articulate enough to explain exactly what those ideals are, rather than just the typical spook stories of sacrifices and criminal cartels."

AS IF TO PROVIDE an object lesson to reinforce the importance of his recent ordination, a few days later, Manson came face-to-face with the indignant wrath of one organized religion. Concerned officials at the Delta Center in Salt Lake City, Utah, had caught wind of the content of Manson's shows, and sent representatives to see the group's Las Vegas show two days earlier, on October 16. The Delta Center found the performance objectionable on several points (Manson's rubber phallus bothered them especially), and informed Marilyn

Manson and Nine Inch Nails that they'd have to make modifications. Both bands consented.

But when the NiN entourage rolled into town, they were greeted with a new surprise. Reznor and company would be allowed to perform under the agreed conditions. But unless Marilyn Manson met with even further demands—which according to a radio report included altering lyrics, remaining silent in between numbers, and not selling any of their confrontational tour merchandise—they were forbidden to play (although they'd be paid in full).

Rather than completely bastardize their set, Marilyn Manson didn't go on. But then, during the Nine Inch Nails set, Trent invited up on stage the newly ordained Reverend Manson, who hopped up clutching a copy of the Book of Mormon. Reznor read a letter to the audience detailing why Marilyn Manson weren't being permitted to perform, and offered his own comments. Manson tossed in a few asides of his own, then began to rend pages from the sacred text, incanting, "He loves me, he loves me not . . . fuck him!" before hurling the spine into the crowd. While the reverend went off and trashed their dressing room, Reznor concluded his set with a stream of obscenities decrying Salt Lake City mayor Deedee Corrandini, the Delta Center, and the Church of Jesus Christ of Latter-day Saints.

What the good folks of Salt Lake City didn't seem to realize was that by barring Manson, they'd basically played into his hands. Their actions blurred the distinction between church and state so glaringly that anyone who'd been paying attention to Manson's detailed harangues on how organized religion was fundamentally money-driven must have smiled. "If there weren't places like Salt Lake City, where they want to ban you, I wouldn't exist," he reminded *Seconds* readers.

The reaction in the local press in the days that followed proved almost as absurd as the events themselves. "Dropping Marilyn Manson from last Tuesday's bill of fare was not an assault on anybody's civil liberties, as some have tried to suggest. Rather, it was an exercise in good taste, something that should be exercised more often if society is ever to banish violence, vulgarity and other depravity to the fringes where it belongs," went an editorial in the *Tribune*. "If Marilyn Manson wants to purvey some kind of political message with its music, its members can always put out a record or get a gig in the underground where their filth won't infect impressionable teenagers." But by preventing the crowd (estimated at ten thousand, with an average age of sixteen) from hearing Marilyn Manson, the Salt Lake City authorities had done more to pique the young people's interest than the actual show (which still wasn't wowing the vast majority) could have.

"The less fuss made, the better. If something is banned, it becomes attractive," noted editor Bryan Gray in Bountiful's *Davis County Clipper*, proving that not all denizens of the Beehive State were shortsighted. And as he also pointed out, the same week NiN and Manson were condemned, Utah residents were welcoming the Rolling Stones—composers of "Sympathy for the Devil"—with open arms.

"Nine Inch Nails and Marilyn Manson's lyrics are about the real world, and what people my age are going through. How do people know what is in my best interest when they don't know me?" wrote young Sarah Padilla of Layton in the pages of Ogden's *Standard-Examiner*. She echoed a sentiment Manson had already voiced to parents repeatedly: Raise your kids better, or Marilyn Manson will raise them instead. "And what we know is that isn't so bad, because I want to raise kids in truth and tell them that everything is a lie." So pick the one that works best for you.

And amid all this furor, an ocean away the release of *POAAF* was being discussed on no less esteemed a floor than that of the British Parliament, where members (in tandem with the Church of England) were calling for a ban on the album's release. MP John Blackburn, the sort to run to the tabloids when he smelled free publicity, called the album "an outrage against society." The fact that outraging society was exactly the point of Manson's music seemed to elude Blackburn's faculties. "It's appalling. I would ban this sort of thing tomorrow. It's breaking up society. It's disgraceful that they're capitalizing on the Manson case." John Tovar of TCA, Manson's management, confirmed that they were having "a lot of problems getting it out over there," in *Jam*, then added, "but we love it anyway." Meanwhile *Kerrang!*, the UK's most prominent heavy metal magazine, awarded *POAAF* the highest marks possible in their publication.

The tour continued through Texas and the Midwest before winding up on the band's home turf in Florida. At the November 20 show at the Arena in Miami, Manson, who'd long espoused freedom to explore sexuality and gender roles as part of the Marilyn Manson doctrine, decided to put his money where his mouth was. Or rather, vice versa.

Only thirteen scheduled dates remained on the "Self Destruct" tour, and the groups had entered what Manson later described to *Alternative Press* as "the end-of-the tour period where bands are like playing pranks on one another, making a spectacle." Nine Inch Nails guitarist Robin Finck, who'd become increasingly close to Twiggy in particular, sauntered out on stage during Manson's set this fateful evening, looking to make mischief and acting lewd. "But instead of being made a fool of, I embraced the situation: I grabbed him and pulled his pants down and sucked his dick." In reality, Finck wasn't wearing pants, just an S&M slave boy rig that exposed his genitalia.

Adding fuel to the fire, no doubt, was the fact that Hugh and Barbara Warner (Ma and Pa Manson, as it were) had turned up to see their boy in action. But apparently they handled it all remarkably well; Manson even claims to have introduced his father to Finck after the show, and that the two shook hands. "My mom is my biggest fan, and my father is always supportive. Maybe it's because they feel responsible for the way I turned out," he chuckled to NiN makeup artist Carol Leggett in an interview for *Paper*. They opted not to dwell on the fact that their only child had engaged another grown man in fellatio in front of thousands of screaming teenagers. "Let's just say the subject never came up at the dinner table."

In the press, Manson had been deliberately cagey concerning his sexual preference. "I've done stuff with guys before," he later insisted to the gay and lesbian newsmagazine *OUT*, "but I wouldn't say that I was gay." And looking at things from the opposite perspective, his fondness for women didn't qualitatively brand him straight. However, when the Finck incident came up the next time he spoke to *Seconds* (who in the past had simply assumed he was a practicing bisexual, based on his rhetoric), he seemed a little skittish. "I don't ever try and put a label on anything," he pointed out. "But I technically felt that, since I didn't have a hard-on, that it only made him gay, my sucking his dick."

But he also acknowledged he could see why people were so uncomfortable with such actions. "People's real fears start to come out when you do something like that," he told *JAM*. "A lot of macho guys started calling me 'faggot,' wanted to start a fight with me. Why would they want to fight me because I did that? Obviously, it scared them. I'm confident enough with my sexuality where I can do something like that. Anyone who knows me knows that I like girls."

The tour wrapped up with scattered dates along the East Coast before beginning a three-night stint at Madison Square Garden, which due to cancellations was reduced to a single show, on December 9. But the next night, Twiggy (quickly becoming the second most popular member of the band with the fans) had his own chance to shine in a different light.

Throughout the tour, Twiggy and Robin Finck had gotten into the habit of jamming on an assortment of classic metal tunes during their down time. Eventually, they confessed their mutual love of Twisted Sister, the cross-dressing Long Island metal quintet who'd scored a double platinum album with their 1984 opus *Stay Hungry*, crowned by the hit "We're Not Gonna Take It." During their heyday, lead singer Dee Snider, who was now fronting the outfit Widowmaker, had even spoken in the hallowed halls of the nation's Capitol against the censorial practices of Tipper Gore and the Parents Music Resource Council. Between the music and Snider's convictions, he seemed a perfect match for the young bucks. They started learning their entire repertoire, and when they decided to do a live show of all Twisted Sister covers, they knew who had to front their little group. They called Dee Snider.

"He thought it was a joke and took a week of convincing," Twiggy admitted to *Seconds*. But eventually, he believed them. And on December 10, at the Rock Ridge Saloon in Manhattan, a select audience bore witness to the only show by Sick Mutha Fuckers. The quartet consisted of Snider, Ramirez, and Finck (for whom Twiggy had actually filled in at the previous night's NiN gig, due to illness), rounded out with Finck's old pal Mike Allen (of the Goodies) banging on the skins.

Devotees got another glimpse at Manson's unique twist on sexuality when the *Seconds* staffers revealed that they'd run into him at the Vault, a Manhattan S and M club, during his visit to New York. With his lanky Morticia Adams locks and trailing pink faux fur coat, many merely mistook the singer for another one of downtown's outrageous transgender elite. They reported that Manson was transfixed watching a man poised on a bench, under a spotlight, jerking off and making faces of ecstasy. He went over and knelt beside the exhibitionist, and picked his brain for a while. "I just wanted to find out what was on his mind. I have to admit, he seemed to have his shit together," he informed his colleagues. "I can see where he's coming from."

By his own admission in the same pages, Manson felt that sex was highly impersonal. "I'm not even sure if I like sex, because I often find myself thinking about masturbating while I'm having sex. It's very strange. I'm starting to think that masturbation is the true form of sex."

The next evening, December 11, was the final night of the tour, at the Spectrum in Philadelphia. The pranks and tricks Manson had alluded to before were about to come to a head, and Nine Inch Nails had decided to revere the time-honored tradition of the headlining act hazing the opener in spades. When Manson emerged from the bathroom, ready to go on stage, he ran smack into two naked girls, kissing and caressing each other. And beside them was an equally naked male subject. Everybody from Nine Inch Nails and Marilyn Manson was sitting on pins and needles, waiting to see what would happen.

"The naked guy says to me, 'I know you've mentioned on stage before that if anyone would come up here you would put your fist in them and I would like to know if you would fist fuck me,'" Manson revealed to *Seconds*. "Assuming that everyone would think I would back down—because that was the joke—I of course said I would do it just to destroy their plans of making a fool out of me." Obviously enjoying enough familiarity with fist-fucking etiquette to know the rules, he donned a big rubber glove that covered the length of his forearm, then smeared his hand in butter and honored the gentleman's request.

But this was only the beginning of the mayhem. As they headed out, the Nails ambushed them, dousing them in baby powder and salsa (which couldn't have looked too different to the crowd from their regular visages), and forcing them to perform covered in goo. Then halfway through their set, a group of male strippers suddenly trotted out on stage and started antagonizing the band with their undulations. Now Manson was getting aggravated, "because I didn't want the crowd to think that was something I had organized because we would never represent our band in such a ridiculous way." He yelled at the strippers to leave, and promoted the crowd to do the same. "I incited a bit of hatred and there was a lot of derogatory comments made towards the sexuality of the male strippers."

They finished the set, and Manson crawled off, clad in little more than a pair of leather shorts and wet socks. Already a sopping wet shambles of beer, sweat, salsa, and Johnson & Johnson, the exiting musicians were suddenly accosted with streams of whipped cream. Before they knew what was happening, security guards handcuffed their hands behind their backs and forced them into the back of a pickup truck. The vehicle pulled off with the trussed-up quintet in back, and proceeded to drive half an hour away from the venue. In the middle of crime-heavy downtown Philadelphia, the kidnappers deposited Marilyn Manson, threw the keys to the handcuffs into an nearby garbage can, tossed a single dollar bill at them, and announced, "Find your way home!"

"It was about twenty-five degrees out and we were all wet and freezing and I was pretty much naked," Manson moaned to *Seconds*. "We looked like a bunch of extras from a John Waters movie." Mercifully, a group of college kids happened upon them and decided to play good Samaritans, driving them back to the venue. In a fitting twist of fate, Manson didn't have to seek vindication, because Reznor had imbibed a bit too heavily before going on, and turned in a sub-standard show, with everyone on stage falling all over one another. "We ended up doing five thousand dollars' worth of damage to our dressing room but I guess the record label has to pay for that."

Six

WITH THEIR FIRST NATIONAL tour under their garters, Marilyn Manson returned to Florida for some well-earned rest and relaxation. But within two weeks, they were in hot water again. The quintet was booked to play a four-date minitour headlining of regional clubs. The first show was scheduled for Jacksonville, Florida, on December 27, at the Club Five. But the moral guardians of Jacksonville weren't exactly hot on the idea of Manson coming to town. Protests from the Christian Coalition had already been expressed in a press conference covered extensively in the December 2 edition of Jacksonville's *Florida Times-Union.*

The right-wing group's displeasure went back to the Nine Inch Nails/Marilyn Manson/Jim Rose Circus Sideshow date at the Jacksonville Coliseum back on November 18. "We have to realize that there were 14- to 18-year-olds at that concert and they were all worked into a frenzy by a band preaching hate and preaching killing," claimed Max Karrer, coordinator of the Christian Coalition of Duval County. Echoing the protestations heard earlier in Salt Lake City, he insisted this was not a matter of free speech. "You don't have the right to yell fire in a crowded movie theater and you shouldn't be able to entice people to hate and kill." (What Karrer overlooked was that one does have a right to yell "fire" if you perceive a potential threat to those in attendance, which is exactly how Manson views the relationship between organized religion and his fans and his band.) Sergeant Larry Sparkman of the vice squad, who'd attended at Karrer's invitation, detailed the more salacious moments from Manson's November set, including the unveiling of the black rubber phallus.

A photo of Karrer appeared alongside the text. In the picture, he holds up the infamous KILL GOD / KILL YOUR MOM & DAD / KILL YOURSELF shirt. What wasn't evident in the shot was the full text printed on the shirt: "Warning: The music of Marilyn Manson contains messages that will KILL GOD in your impressionable teenage minds. As a result you could be convinced to KILL YOUR MOM & DAD and eventually in an act of hopeless rock and roll behavior you will KILL YOURSELF. Please burn your records while there is still hope." Having missed the humor and deeper meaning in the shirt's message, Mr. Karrer could only have hoped to lend some of the band's shock value to his own crusade by displaying it.

Manson didn't discourage the Christian Coalition from lodging their protests. "They have every right to say that we shouldn't perform in your town," he parried, "as much as we have a right to come to that town." He'd heard rumors before the Nine Inch Nails gig that he might be arrested following his performance, but hadn't made any noticeable changes, and managed to escape any consequences. But in the interim, the Coalition (in conjunction with the Jacksonville police, according to Manson) had let the band know that they would attempt to stop the show.

Although Manson had mentioned pointedly in the press on several occasions that the band's shows were wholly spontaneous, he made a point of speaking with the manager of the Club Five. He asked if he should have any special concerns about that evening's show, any unique circumstances he might want to take into account. He was assured that everything would be fine, and that all they expected was for the band to turn in their usual performance.

Fans had come to expect explicit content from a Marilyn Manson show, but they didn't get much on December 27. "I felt that that night, however, was pretty tame in comparison to some nights I've had on stage," Manson told *Seconds*. Regardless, as soon as he exited the stage, vice squad goons, who had been waiting in his dressing room, arrested him. The whole affair seemed a little too convenient for Manson. "They had been waiting for me and I was pretty much convicted before I got there." Suspiciously, the same club manager who'd told him not to be concerned wasn't arrested, although technically he should've been. Authorities described the bust as part of "an undercover adult entertainment investigation."

Manson was charged with violating the Adult Entertainment Code. But what exactly transpired? Well, according to the police report, "During the concert [Mr. Manson] pulled down his pants exposing a simulated black penis and began to rubb [*sic*] it. He squeezed it several times and pulled down his pants exposing his buttocks and made no attempt to pull his pants up." And Manson had company in the paddy wagon. The fuzz had also taken offense at the actions of Jack Off Jill's Jessicka, who was nailed for contributing to lewdness after inviting a man up on stage to display his testicles.

The police took Manson downtown, where he was strip-searched and harassed about his appearance. One officer purportedly suggested he remove his lip ring, lest it get torn out in some sort of unforeseeable mishap during his visit to the clink, and there was plenty of hearty speculation made about his sexual orientation. Fortunately, when he finally landed behind bars, his fellow inmates proved remarkably cool. Nobody got the bright idea of trying to make the new kid their bitch. "It was after a show and I had a lot of lipstick on my face and looked like some sort of undead prostitute," he reminded *Seconds*. He was eventually released on $1,500 bail, after spending sixteen hours languishing in the arms of the law. Although he managed to avoid a court appearance, the Christian Coalition seemed to have achieved victory. Manson vowed never to play Jacksonville again.

Operating on absolutely no sleep, Manson hurried on to the next evening's gig in Orlando, determined to thwart the efforts of Jacksonville's finest to keep him from playing the show. But the Jacksonville cops also made sure they got on the horn to their counterparts in Fort Lauderdale, where the group was scheduled to wrap up the minitour on New Year's Eve. Filled with trepidation that a repeat performance, or possibly even something worse at the hands of the Fort Lauderdale boys in blue, awaited him, Manson went ahead and did the full show as usual. For their encore, they served up a scorching rendition of Patti Smith's "Rock & Roll Nigger," which he dedicated to the Jacksonville police and the Christian Coalition. "It was kind of ironic, because we had just started to do that Patti Smith song and I thought it became very relevant to my reality after that happened because of getting fucked with for the way I look." Then, for the grand finale, he set fire to Old Glory, and told everyone to fuck off.

ALTHOUGH MTV AND RADIO had roundly ignored "Get Your Gunn," Marilyn Manson valiantly forged ahead and released a new single, "Lunchbox." The six-track CD version included four remixes of the title tune, including a cleaned-up radio version (the "High-school Drop-outs" mix). But of greater interest to most fans was the non-LP selection "Down in the Park." Produced by Reznor, and featuring Twiggy on bass, the track offered up Marilyn Manson's take on a song originally written and recorded by UK synthpop star Gary Numan, who'd had a Top Ten hit in America in 1980 with "Cars." Taken from Numan's 1979 album *Replicas* (which went number one in England), the song bristled with an air of detachment and repressed xenophobia that fit in perfectly with Manson's own material. Not that they opted to stick too close to the blueprint. "It's very different from my original, isn't it?" laughed Numan when asked about it in 1997.

The infamous Richard Kern, a thirty-nine-year-old NYC fetish shutterbug and filmmaker, directed the accompanying video. Kern's credits already included clips for Sonic Youth ("Death Valley '69," "Money Love"), King Missile ("Detachable Penis"), and Cop Shoot Cop, as well as the notorious *Hardcore: The Films of Richard Kern, Vols. 1 and 2*, star-studded with gruesome performances from the likes of Lydia Lunch and Jim Thirlwell (aka Foetus). The video had been shot on a ninety-degree weekend in September, in between "Self

Destruct" dates. Manson wasn't feeling too hot that day, although he offered to let a writer from *Film Threat Video Guide* on the scene help himself to the fifth of Jack Daniel's under the seat of his car. "I drink a bottle a day on tour," he claimed, "except my sinuses are blocked up today."

The concept, dreamed up by Manson and Kern, centered around six-year-old Robert Pierce, star of MM stage and studio efforts ("My Monkey"). The boy represents the youthful Manson, who gets bullied on the way to the roller rink, toting his metal lunch box. After breaking free, he vows to get even with his tormentors. He shaves his head into a fetching mohawk, destroys the lunch box, and grows up to become a prominent rock star. The video's final image is of a *Rambo* lunch box—the last lunch box design to be mass-produced in metal—going up in flames.

The shoot prompted Manson to recollect less pleasant moments from his own childhood for *Film Threat Video Guide*. Manson reckoned that young Pierce bore an unpleasant resemblance to a freckle-faced lad who'd beaten him up at school. "Mike Bernhardt was the kid who used to wait at the bus stop for me when I was attending school in Ohio." He went on to speculate that Mr. Bernhardt had wound up in a trailer park somewhere close to the homestead. "Well, that's what happened to most of the kids I grew up with."

ON JANUARY 11, 1995, they were on the road again. At the Abyss in Houston, Texas, they kicked off a headlining tour scheduled to last exactly two months, with an almost forty-show agenda. For their opening act they'd enlisted Monster Voodoo Machine, a seven-piece ensemble from Toronto whose blend of hard rock riffs, beats, and samples seemed complementary. But by the very second show, the band found itself at the center of yet another controversy. To quote Dorothy Parker, "What fresh hell was this?"

Like many bands, Marilyn Manson's tour rider (an amendment to their standard contract, stipulating conditions the venue had to provide for the band, most notably the musical and PA equipment on stage, and the types of food and drink in the dressing rooms) included a few items intended mainly in jest. From exotic flavors of animal jerky to nubile groupies with 36-D cups *and* genius IQs, the requests artists place just to amuse and/or inconvenience club managers are legion. Marilyn Manson's hospitality and technical rider at this time was surprisingly reasonable: the usual assortment of meats and cheeses, Jack Daniel's and a case of Budweiser, gum, cigarettes, and clean towels (Manson's once-beloved Caramello bars, however, had now been replaced with Reese's peanut butter cups). But among the sillier items listed were a can of spray cheese, glitter, and one "live chicken (female)."

The nightclub Trees apparently took the business of riders very seriously, because someone had provided the poultry. And when Manson went on stage, the caged bird was right there with them. That much everyone agrees on. But from there, stories diverge. Over the course of the next few weeks, the argument raged back in forth in the pages of local rag *The Met* over just what had occurred that night.

Some versions have Manson deliberately freeing the chicken and tossing it into the crowd, while others claim he accidentally kicked open the cage and the bird escaped. Regardless, it somehow ended up in the clutches of the frenzied audience. From there, according to a letter sent in by Karen Davis of Potomac, Maryland's United Poultry Concerns, "members of the audience dismembered the live chicken in a bacchanalian orgy of violence." If this were the case, the band and the venue had violated anticruelty laws on the books in the Lone Star State.

"Music can be a powerful forum for creative expression, including feelings of rage and anger," proclaimed Bill Dollinger of Friends of Animals in Washington, D.C. "Such emotions can easily be expressed without inflicting pain and brutal death upon non-willing participants."

In actuality, what apparently happened was a local culinary whiz saw the bird darting through the crowd, and told a friend that if he caught the bird, the chef would be delighted to fricassee the hen. The pal pursued the poultry into the mosh pit, and caught it, but another audience member came forward and pleaded for the bird's life. A contest of tug-of-chicken ensued, in the process of which many feathers were shed, which to audience members might have presented the illusion of the chicken being shredded by impassioned fans. But according to the story as recounted by editors of *The Met*, the chicken was confiscated. Whether it was returned to the band, nobody knows.

Over the course of the next few months, animal rights group PeTA (People for the Ethical Treatment of Animals) also joined the fray and protested any further (ab)use of live chickens on stage. (Although when contacted to comment on the events at Trees, a PeTA spokesperson admitted they'd never found conclusive evidence that the animal had been harmed, and thus hadn't taken specific action regarding the rumors.) Manson pointed out that the band had a six-year-old child up on stage with them under more perverse circumstances. "And my point to PeTA was, 'Where were you when this kid was onstage?' Which I think is a bigger concern than an animal used for McChicken sandwiches," he complained to *Alternative Press*. He hypothesized that people concerned with such causes were splitting hairs over issues of "morality" to avoid delving deeper into their own prejudices and shortcomings. "I happen to like animals, you know, I have pets, but at the same time that kind of fanatical reaction to having a chicken in a cage—I think these people could probably spend their time doing more important things—bombing abortion clinics, for example."

Eventually the band stopped having caged chickens on stage altogether, although authorities tipped off by animal activists still periodically checked up on them. Finally, a year later, Manson snapped and retaliated. "I wrote them a letter saying, 'Each time I hear our name brought up in association with PeTA, I'm going to torture an animal in the privacy of my own home.' We haven't heard from them since."

But now the wheels were set in motion, and the rallying cry "Kill the Chicken" would soon become yet another puzzle piece in the convoluted Marilyn Manson mythology. (One fan created a memorable banner to be unfurled at shows that read KILL GOD / KILL YOUR MOM & DAD / KILL YOURSELF / KILL THE CHICKEN, and purportedly an unfinished song called "Kill the Chicken" was heard at a handful of sound checks.) As Pogo observed, the chicken had now simply become a symbol for the band's larger ideas. "To kill the chicken does not mean to literally kill a chicken, but it has become a metaphor for a much greater cause related to smashing everything that deserves to be smashed," he expounded to the *Gaston Gazette*. Folks who wanted to "kill the chicken" had announced their resolve not to tolerate the bland, the mediocre, or the spineless.

THE TOUR CONTINUED THROUGH Texas and on to California. At the January 19 show at the Whiskey in Los Angeles, Mr. Manson opted to flash his real johnson, instead of the big black stunt double. "He sashayed around the stage, pulled down his tight black leather trousers, mooned and waved his rather small penis at the crowd," reported the on-line music bulletin *Addicted to Noise*. He also smeared his face with lipstick, announcing, "I have to look pretty because I'm in Hollywood." But a minute later he berated the crowd for being "a bunch of fags," and then scrawled the offending slur on his chest in lipstick just to underscore the point. After the gig, members of the ensemble retired to DragonFly on Santa Monica Boulevard, where Twiggy was sighted putting the moves on the lovely Sean Yseult of White Zombie.

January 24 found the group back in Seattle, where they once again crossed paths with Veronica Kirchoff. She'd scheduled a follow-up interview to follow the band's sound check at Moe's, but when she arrived "the only person who was there was Sara Lee Lucas." Eventually the others sauntered in, but she hesitated to approach them. The band went through their paces, and during "Down in the Park," Manson caught sight of her. He finished the song and came over to chat. "I just sat there and talked to him for a while, but it wasn't a formal interview." She hung out with him after the show that night, and when they parted ways he promised to keep in touch . . . again. "I kept sending him stuff as I did it," she sighs, "but I never heard anything back from him."

From Washington, the tour continued up to Vancouver, then

continued through the Midwest, back up to Toronto, and down through New England. By the time they hit the Big Apple, playing the Limelight on February 12, a month of shows had tightened their set into enough of a spectacle to shock even jaded New Yorkers. "I've been to hardcore shows, punk shows, metal thrash shows and goth shows, but I don't think any of them added up to the intensity of the performance I saw by Marilyn Manson," wrote Myke Hideous in the *Aquarian Weekly*. Just moments after chiding the fans not to stage-dive, lest they incur the consequences, Manson plucked a crowd surfer up onto the stage during "Sweet Dreams," held him down on his back in a sacrificial spread, and "serenaded" him, before throwing the little fish back into the roiling throng. Manson also endeared himself to fans nightly by singling out audience members and inquiring, "Who do you want to fuck?" The correct response being an adoring "I want to fuck *you*, Daddy," directed back at the reverend. "Marilyn Manson is one of the best shows I've seen since the Plasmatics in the mid-'80s," concluded Hideous. A dubious distinction, and not entirely an appropriate comparison, but a remarkable compliment nevertheless. But he didn't note that tensions between the singer and drummer Sara Lee Lucas seemed to be running extremely high, prompting a volley of water bottles and drumsticks between the two throughout the set.

The run up and down the East Coast for the remaining half of the tour wound up in the Carolinas for the last three dates. Paula O'Keefe had traveled down from Maryland to catch the wrap-up, starting with the gig at Ziggy's Tavern, in Winston-Salem, North Carolina, on March 9. O'Keefe had already seen the "Get Your Gunn" video on MTV, and been distinctly unimpressed. "I was like, 'Oh brother, another noise band with a grudge against society. . . . Big deal, I've heard this before,' " recounts the forty-two-year-old. "I listened to the Stooges, I listened to Bowie. . . . I've been through this." But her roommates Liz Bouras and Judy Pope had become smitten with *POAAF*, and after seeing the Manson show at the 9:30 Club in Washington, D.C. on February 14, they had insisted that O'Keefe check out the band live.

Having driven down from the D.C. metro area, the trio arrived to find what O'Keefe describes as "a dive-y little roadhouse made out of plastic sheeting and two-by-fours." Even though six electric heaters were suspended from the ceiling for warmth, the club was freezing cold. The band was running almost three hours late because the police had decided to pop by and introduce themselves to Manson. "Basically they'd been getting the third degree from the local authorities, telling them what they could not do on stage," she laughs. "You're in Jesse Helms country down there."

By the time they finally came out, O'Keefe was so chilly and cranky that nothing less than a full-fledged musical epiphany was going to endear her to Manson. Miraculously, they didn't let her down. "In about four minutes, I completely forgot that I was cold, that it was late, that I hadn't liked their album. They completely blew my brains out." O'Keefe was excited to see the next two shows, simply because she was so taken with Manson's live performance. What she couldn't anticipate was that both would go down in the Spooky Kids annals as exceptionally memorable dates.

The mood in Carrboro, North Carolina, was already pretty wacky before Marilyn Manson even pulled into city limits. They'd canceled a scheduled February 16 gig at the same venue, Cat's Cradle. And their advance publicity wasn't exactly positive. A show preview published in the *North Carolina News and Observer* had included testimony from Steve Adair, a twenty-nine-year-old roadie for death metal bands who'd caught the MM show in Ohio earlier, and was dismayed. The article also incorporated anecdotes from a seventeen-year-old Charles Manson fan; a New York executive from Columbia Records (and admitted "shock rock" fan); and twenty-two-year-old student Jeff Leagan, who claimed "their music works out aggression and all the frustration of going to work during the week and putting up with everything." But Leagan also expressed concern about "homosexual themes" he'd noted in the group's set at the Mad Monk on February 20. The article went on to mention that Leagan's girlfriend, twenty-three-year-old Tracy King, had been knocked unconscious after stage-diving at the Wilmington, North Carolina, show.

As Paula O'Keefe had noted the night before, the crowd once

again was composed predominantly of young teenagers. "You have to grin at that," she writes. "For appreciation you want college kids, but for fanaticism, hysteria, wild deeds of danger and devotion, you want junior high. And here it is." This evening, the set ran smoothly, including "Sweet Dreams," during which Manson shattered a hand-held lamp against his chest. During "Lunchbox," Manson got out his trusty supply of butane as usual. But tonight his firebug tendencies got out of hand, and he set Lucas's drum kit ablaze for the grand finale . . . with the drummer still seated behind it. Blocked in by the flames, the drummer managed to escape with singed hair but otherwise relatively unharmed.

What Manson had apparently forgotten (or overlooked) before destroying Lucas's instrument was that they still had one additional rescheduled date to play, at Alcatrazz, in Columbia, South Carolina. From the start, things didn't bode well. The venue was a dance club, complete with synchronized lights and disco ball. Many of those in attendance hadn't turned up to see Marilyn Manson; they were just killing time before the Saturday night dance party started.

To compound matters, Manson had decided to perpetuate what O'Keefe calls "the Curse of the Tour's Last Night," and do unto Monster Voodoo Machine as NiN had done unto them. During MVM's set, the Manson road crew summarily doused the Canadian ensemble with eggs, flour, tomatoes, and vinegar. "Got the makings of a complete Greek salad up here," cracked singer Adam Sewell. But they got their licks in, too, with Adam mercilessly mimicking Mr. Manson onstage with alarming accuracy. By the end of their set, the scattered Manson fans were in stitches; combined with the largely disinterested crowd of disco bunnies, the atmosphere was shot to hell.

And apparently, someone had tipped MVM off to what was in store that evening, for they'd already concocted their own revenge, inspired by the poultry pandemonium in Dallas two months prior. Even as the staff tried to clean up the mess on stage, other agents were strategically positioning chicken fryer parts all over the stage, on keyboards, between foot pedals. Raw meat was hidden in every conceivable nook and cranny. Since there was no backstage per se, the band had to enter through the crowd. As they made their entrance, the few fans gathered up front could hear the band members muttering and cursing under their breath.

The band launched into their set, but the vibe in the club was negative and stifling, and the poultry debris seriously grossed out the players. Manson hurled pieces of chicken into the crowd, only to have it thrown back at him. Madonna's keyboard failed, and he smashed it into the stage. All the material that Adam Sewell had parodied earlier had been hastily exorcised from the set, leaving holes in the program. The crowd began to turn from nonplussed to hostile, throwing ice cubes, hot dogs, and grimy pieces of chicken at the performers. Manson ripped into "Lunchbox" by hollering, "Next motherfucker's gonna get my chicken," but the players weren't together and had to stop and start over. The mood grew more and more grim.

"That was a truly horrible experience," says O'Keefe, who was transfixed watching Manson's frustration and hurt. "I'm sure it wasn't the first time they'd faced a hostile audience, but it was the first time I'd seen them do it." Although she'd only seen the band twice so far, already she'd begun to appreciate the dynamics of their show. "A lot of what they do really depends on the audience being willing to dive in there and be part of the mystique and the energy. And when they face an audience that laughs at them, Manson finds it very hard to find his ground."

As the set drew to a close, Manson announced that this was the final show of the tour. And he had just the perfect "big finish" in mind. He started clawing at his belly, as if trying to tear out the source of his pain. Then he snatched up a bottle some yahoo had tossed on stage, and smashed it. Holding the jagged edge up against his pale, emaciated stomach, he seem suspended for a moment, lost in contemplation of the pros and cons of committing hara-kiri with a Budweiser. In the end, he thought better of dying in such ignominious surroundings, and settled for merely slicing a long red gash along his torso. The band struggled through the end of the set, and even stuck around for an encore: a cathartic attack on "Helter Skelter."

SEVEN

AS SOON AS THEY got off the road, Sara Lee Lucas handed in his resignation. "[Sara Lee] really wasn't growing with us musically." Manson told Gail Worley. "He was having a hard time keeping up with our lifestyle and our songwriting, so we just split up."

"It was kind of mutual," adds Scott Mitchell concerning the drummer's decision to leave the band. "He really was not carrying his weight as far as playing. And we were all aware of it, and did what we could to help him. And he didn't make the effort to improve. So just looking at it very matter-of-factly, it was strictly for technical reasons. It wasn't much of anything personal."

The band got cracking on finding a new drummer, and soon recruited Frank Wilson into their dark fold. Wilson (who some claim is really named Kenny Borus) was a native of Framingham, Massachusetts, who eventually relocated to "Sin City," Las Vegas. His parents were both thoroughly steeped in show business traditions. His mother was a tap dancer who'd been contracted to the Warner Brothers studio at the tender age of three. His father was a crooner who chummed around with the likes of Paul Anka and Frank Sinatra. In Vegas, little Frank had honed his rock and roll drumming skills, only to learn they were in scant demand. After finishing high school, he hustled briefly as a carny at the extravagant Circus Circus casino. Ultimately, he wearied of the bright lights and roulette table, and relocated to Florida. There he played any gig he could, including an ironic stint pounding skins in the pit of a production of the Andrew Lloyd Webber rock opera *Jesus Christ Superstar*. Eventually, he was recommended to the Manson camp via word of mouth.

Wilson's qualifications fit Manson's diverse requirements. Not only could he beat the hell out of a kit live, but he also knew how to program electronic percussion, having been fascinated with drum machines from the start. "If I didn't know the equipment I would never have been given the opportunity to play with them in the first place, because that's exactly what the band was looking for, to take them to the next level," Wilson told *Drum* magazine. "The old drummer didn't know about machines, so when they were looking for a new drummer, Trent had a lot to say about who they chose. Trent basically said, 'well, I'm the producer, and I want someone who can work with me and my machines.'"

Signing on to the Manson payroll, Wilson assumed the moniker Ginger Fish. The forename was a paean to Ginger Rogers, Hollywood actress and Fred Astaire's best-loved dancing partner. Other theories regarding the attribution of "Ginger" have included the Tina Louise character from *Gilligan's Island*, and porn actress Ginger Lynn. Judy Pope notes that "Ginger himself has suggested famed drummer Ginger Baker [of Cream], but that would miss the point, Baker being male." And while Paul Semel of *huH* once cracked that the Fish portion was a nod to the Abe Vigoda character on the TV shows *Barney Miller* and *Fish*, the reality was much more grisly.

Up until the arrival of Jeffrey Dahmer, Albert Fish was America's most notorious cannibal. He'd been born Hamilton Fish, but he soon began calling himself "Albert" after the kids at school tormented him with the nickname "Ham and Eggs." Albert, like so many other serial killers, was a chronic bed wetter. Fish married a woman nine years younger than he and fathered six kids. Unfortunately for him, his wife ran away with a boarder. When she returned to the family home

Fish was enraged to find out that she was keeping her lover secreted away in the attic. Predictably this provoked a huge argument, and the wife and her man left again.

After his spouse split the nest for good, Albert began having hallucinations, often shaking his fist at the sky and screaming, "I am Christ!" A spanking connoisseur, Fish encouraged his kids and their pals to paddle his behind until he bled. But sometimes that just didn't deliver enough pain, and he soon began inserting needles into his groin (sometimes so deeply that they disappeared for good). Mr. Fish also enjoyed soaking cotton balls in alcohol, shoving them up his rectum, and then lighting them on fire! Naturally, all these atrocities worked up an appetite, which Albert sated by occasionally feasting on human feces.

Albert believed he had been commanded by God to castrate young boys. He traveled across America molesting children of both sexes. Authorities said he was responsible for at least one hundred sexual attacks, but Fish places the number closer to four hundred. He killed for the first time in 1910, but the crime that eventually brought him down didn't occur until 1928. Fish had befriended the Budd family while living in White Plains, New York. On June 3 he told twelve-year-old Grace Budd that she'd been invited to a fictitious birthday party. He volunteered to walk her there, took her to an isolated cottage, and promptly dismembered her body, cooking up a tasty stew from some of the more savory bits. He didn't get caught for this crime, but he wasn't content to leave well enough alone. In 1934, after a couple of psychiatric committals, Fish mailed an anonymous letter to the Budds telling them their daughter was dead, but that they could rest assured that she'd died a virgin. The police traced the letter back to him and he confessed to at least three other child murders.

Fish tried to plead insanity, yet the prosecution provided psychiatric testimony that claimed coprophagy (consuming excrement) is a common trait and not at all proof of insanity; surprisingly, an X ray taken in prison—showing twenty-nine needles implanted in his groin—didn't count for much in court either. Fish was quickly convicted and sentenced to die. Mythology claims that it took two jolts to do the job because the chair was short-circuited by all the needles Al had stuck in his body.

WITHIN TWO WEEKS, THE band was back on the bus. "I prefer to be on the road than to be just sitting somewhere," Manson said in *Livewire*. "Touring is the only thing that makes us feel alive." On March 24, 1995, they headed out as the support act on the second leg of the Danzig tour. And with them was an unheard-of thrash band named Korn.

Glenn Danzig made no bones about his fondness for the Florida five. "Every time I'd meet with the promoters, like the radio people, I'd ask, 'Do you play Manson?' " he recalled in an interview for *Alternative Press*. "And they'd go, 'Oh, we loved the show last night!' "

"Well?"

"We like 'em . . . but we can't play them," would come the reply.

"There are songs on that record you can play," Glenn would contend.

"Well, it's a little edgy . . ."

"I thought you liked the band."

"Well, yeah, they're great . . ." and the circle went round again.

"When we were out with Danzig, we played to a lot of crowds that had a disproportionate amount of kids there to see us," Daisy Berkowitz claimed in *Guitar School*. If Glenn was perturbed by that state of affairs, he didn't let on. "It was really funny when we took them on the road," he admits. "There would be these twelve-and thirteen-year-old girls, with the little lunch pails and white skin and striped tights. It was pretty funny seeing it. But [their show] was not shocking at all. And seeing them doing what they're doing on stage was no different from seeing Iggy or Alice Cooper."

Learning the sets largely via trial by fire, Ginger Fish had the good sense not to repeat Sara Lee Lucas's mistakes. To keep the song tempos strict, he used a click track, and with good reason. "A lot of drummers could save their jobs if they'd learn to play with a click track," he reminded *Drum* readers. "If you play with five individuals who drink or do any kind of weird substances, naturally, some controlled substances make you hyper, some of them make you sluggish. And if you have one person in the band doing an upper and another person in the band doing a downer and drinking, you're going to get that conflict. No matter how good you think you play, you're going to get an argument: 'You sped up on that song.' " With a click track going in his headset, Ginger could avoid (or at least minimize) such conflicts. "I know [a song's tempo] is exactly ninety-eight beats per minute every night, or whatever it is. I play perfectly so that it's the same consistency night after night. Part of being a professional is being consistent."

Ginger was less prepared to deal with Manson's onstage outbursts, fits of violence that he often directed at his drummer. "I don't know how much of it is an act, and how much of it is genuine anger or frustration," Danzig observed. Regardless, Fish quickly learned to like it or lump it.

And Ginger wasn't the only person Manson was abusing. The singer routinely peppered his stage patter by calling the audience "cunts" or "fucks." But he insisted in *Livewire* that he cared deeply for his fans. "I wouldn't say that I dislike them at all. Sometimes I have to get them riled up, so I may call them a few names. I don't think that anyone should take it personally, unless they deserve it."

Verbal abuse wasn't the only trick in his bag either. One tactic that definitely got the crowd's attention was Manson's penchant for spitting on the assembled, and encouraging them to return in kind. "It's not something that I invented or anything like that," he responded when *Generation* suggested some people might take offense at the practice. He claimed it was practically subconscious at this point, but pointed out that the gesture did have special significance. "It's meant to be a powerful form of expression. A lot of ancient cultures used it in their witchcraft and black magic. On stage it's like a bonding thing with the crowd." And it wasn't a one-way street; he wanted to be spat on, too. "It's an interaction between energy and bodily fluid. A lot of people get pissed off about it, but if they do, they shouldn't come."

"A lot of what I say to our fans is, 'Stop worrying about trying to fit into the status quo of what is beautiful and what is politically correct. Believe in yourself and stick to what's right. If you wanna be like me, then be like yourself,' " he later elaborated in *Rolling Stone*. "It's the whole Nietzsche philosophy of you are your own God. That's why I debase myself in the concerts and tell fans to spit on me. I'm saying to them, 'You are no different from me.' "

And then there were the regular cheerleading sessions where he'd incite the crowd to chant "We hate love / We love hate" at the top of their lungs. "I like doing that," he confessed in an interview for an unfinished documentary. "I don't think people express their hatred enough. They need to let that out. Political correctness has really suppressed hatred. Which in a sense is good. I've got no problem with that. I don't want everyone going around killing each other. That's not my message. But there's no reason to be ashamed to express a natural human feeling, which is hatred.

"You need balance," he continued. "It can't be all love-love-love . . . and it can't be all hate-hate-hate for me, either. Love and hate are exactly the same thing. It's a strong emotion. I have a hard time saying I hate a lot of things, because I have a hard time saying I love a lot of things. It's exactly the same. Accidentally I might say I hate something. But what I'd rather say, what I mean to say is, I dislike it. Or I don't have time for it. I don't care about it. The word 'hate' gets misused a lot, too. People don't appreciate its value."

But as Paula O'Keefe had observed at the final show of the previous tour, the act that upset crowds the most was Manson's forays into self-mutilation on stage. "The first time I did it, a couple years ago, it was by accident," he insisted to *huH*. "I got pissed off and smashed a bottle on myself, and it tore me up. I didn't feel it, and I was like, 'this is strange.' " But from then on, his routine attacks on the pale flesh of his skinny torso were wholly intentional.

"It was a bit symbolic, on one level, because in front of an audience I see it as being ritualistic," he expounded. He called the ritual "very old, and very powerful," comparing it to the rush of the ancient Romans feeding Christians to the lions, or Hitler leading the Nuremberg rallies, the crowd hanging on his every word. "It's the interaction between one person and a lot of others who are listening to that person." Acknowledging that power would become an important theme in the new songs Manson was writing, but in the meantime, he felt the self-mutilation could be viewed on several levels: "To see people's reactions, to see how that affected them, to show that I meant what I was saying. It was also careless abandon." Eventually he would largely abandon the practice, but not until he'd made a map of his own body. "I look at the scars that I have and they line up with the experiences that I went through to get to where I'm at," he reflected. "I look at it as a stage of evolution, or decay—whichever it may be."

But as Dr. Armando Favazza, a professor of psychiatry at the University of Missouri–Columbia Medical School observed in a 1997 *New York Times Magazine* article on the practice of self-mutilation, as many as two million (or more) Americans, mostly teenage girls, shared Manson's need to inflict harm on themselves in such a fashion. "People harm themselves because it makes them feel better; they use physical pain to obfuscate a deeper, more intolerable psychic pain associated with feelings of anger, sadness or abandonment," wrote the story's author, Jennifer Egan. "Often the injury is used to relieve the pressure or hysteria these emotions can cause. . . . It can also jolt people out of states of numbness and emptiness—it can make them feel alive." If Manson's music was fueled by the unpleasantness that had surrounded him since childhood, revisiting those memories nightly could only prompt more and more outrageous reactions.

Naturally, all these extreme onstage antics had repercussions for the road crew. "Someone's constantly havin' to stitch me up from stage wounds, finding us prescription narcotics for pain and things like that, so we tend to put ourselves through hell and back." Manson told *PM* magazine. "When I get onstage, I really let myself go, so whatever happens, happens.

"For me, to be on stage is an outlet to release all the emotions I've pent up all day, whether that be aggression, or anything I might be feeling that day," he added. "I tend to save that all up, so it becomes real explosive."

And while the band was racking up their share of triumphs, Manson definitely had his share of problems to deal with, on whatever level. On March 30, during an interview, Manson let slip that after three and a half years together, he'd just split up with his girlfriend, Melissa Romero. She had read in *Seconds* that Manson and actress Traci Lords were sleeping together, and didn't take the news well. And once again, when pressed on the issue of whether or not his relationship with the former teen porn queen was sexual, the singer turned slippery. "Not necessarily," he told North Dakota's *Rage*. "I met her after a show in Los Angeles, and we had a lot in common. We're both misperceived by a lot of people, and we became close friends. People don't respect her for what she's done. I had a lot of sympathy for her. She seems to have a hard time dealing with her misperceptions, whereas mine don't bother me as much."

The controversial nature of Manson's music and stage show once again prompted threats of cancellation, this time when the quintet were gearing up for a homecoming of sorts, at the James A. Rhodes Arena in Akron, Ohio, less than thirty miles to the north of the former Warner homestead in Canton. After reading an interview with Mr. Manson published in the *Beacon Journal*'s *Enjoy! Magazine* a few days earlier, certain locals began demanding the cancellation of the show scheduled for Sunday, April 23. According to the *Beacon Journal*, Manson told their reporter his onstage antics included torturing animals, self-mutilation, and real and simulated sex, sometimes with audience members.

"I'm very concerned that an institution like Akron University would allow that to be displayed in our community, that people could actually have a chance to see that and say they saw it in Akron," complained Sheila Thomack, director of Christian education for Redeemer Lutheran Church in Cuyahoga Falls. The same article also included comments from concerned parents and their children, including the wisdom of thirteen-year-old Jeremy Fisher, "who prefers Hootie & the Blowfish, Pearl Jam and Stone Temple Pilots." "People who like that music are a bunch of sickos," admonished young Fisher. "It's a bad impression for young people and the school."

When the press tracked the former Brian Warner down in his hotel room in Detroit, he responded with a benevolence that would only increase over the next few months. He claimed that he preferred a homecoming surrounded with controversy, because it revealed that the community actually cares: "It shows parents are at least taking some time and concern to look into the social lives of their children. But I'm not necessarily saying they're right." The hysteria only served to prove the points he was trying to make, "that parents don't really take the time to raise their kids except after a big mess occurs and they want to try to point their fingers at someone else and blame them for the way their kids grew up."

But as the *Beacon Journal*'s Kevin C. Johnson, also noted, Manson had already performed in northeast Ohio several times in the previous year, including two sold-out shows with NiN. And at none of those concerts had Manson displayed the behavior the community was wringing its hands over. "At best, his band's opening set was creepy, but its most memorable aspect was the presence of Mr. Manson." It was simply a case of the Emperor's New Clothes. "I'm only as sick as the person who is thinking about me is," concluded Manson. "When it comes right down to it, Marilyn Manson is just another punk band."

While on his old turf, the Ohio native also took time out to revisit one of the birthplaces of Marilyn Manson: Heritage Christian School. No doubt the sight of the lanky, sinister Manson skulking through the halls sent more than one sister clutching for her rosary. "It was an interesting experience," he confessed to *PM*. "They knew who I was, and I don't think they liked it very much. But I wanted to go back and show them what they had created, and they weren't too happy seeing the job they had done." Even though sales for *Portrait of an American Family* had now passed the one hundred thousand point, Brian Warner's former teachers could hardly view him as a success story.

Community concern manifested itself again at the FM Kirby Center in Wilkes Barre, Pennsylvania, where security precautions for the show were heightened. Two security guards scanned ticket holders with metal detectors, while inside a total of fourteen additional guards roamed the aisles and blocked the stage, which was also separated from the floor audience by a metal barricade. But ultimately, the show proved remarkably conservative. The venue was a restored Art

Deco movie palace, and the owners had even covered the wood stage with a tarpaulin to protect the surface from scuff marks and tape. "Try to imagine the sublime weirdness of your typical Marilyn Manson/Danzig crowd being shown to its red velvet seats by elderly usher ladies with flashlights," noted Paula O'Keefe. The fans stayed in their seats, but Manson tried to liven things up by vaulting the barrier and singing in the orchestra pit briefly, only to be hoisted back on stage by security. He kept displays of nudity to a bare minimum, and there was no self-laceration, but he still didn't charm much of the crowd. "A large number of kids just were not coping with this," observed O'Keefe of the crowd reaction. "This seems to be a very conservative area."

Even with their own coterie of fans in the house, Marilyn Manson had to contend with the fact that Danzig fans were less likely to take to them as kindly as the Nine Inch Nails fans had. In an interview with the *Times Leader*, Manson revealed some interesting insights into the reaction of the Danzig supporters to his onstage exhibitionism, the black rubber phallus, and other provocative antics. "It's a special kind of crowd—testosterone-filled teenage guys," who Manson once again joked all want to have sex with him, "but that makes them uncomfortable so then they want to beat [me up] instead."

After the disasters surrounding their last gig in Jacksonville, Manson could've been forgiven for canceling the show scheduled at Club Five on May 10. "But we felt we didn't want to let down any fans we may have in Jacksonville, so we went ahead and did it," he explained to *The ROC* ("the voice of Rock Out Censorship," who also targeted future Manson foe C. DeLores Tucker in the same issue). Mercifully, their set went almost without a hitch. Yet as fate would have it, right as they launched into their last song, the club's power went out. In the future, Manson would stick to his resolve to avoid Jacksonville.

The tour wrapped up on May 14 at the Edge, in Orlando, Florida. In the end, folks who had harbored aspirations that Danzig and Mr. Manson might bond over their shared affinity for the Church of Satan were disappointed. However, at one East Coast venue, the diminutive but beefy Glenn rescued Mr. Manson, Pogo, and road manager

Frankie Proia after the set. The hired security "thugs" had taken offense at being spat on during the Manson show, and it was up to Danzig, who came out of the shadows swinging a Louisville slugger, to play the cavalry and rescue the trio. But when it came down to forming a long-lasting friendship with the tiny titan, Manson told an interviewer on MTV's *Headbangers' Ball* that "we've been naked with his bus driver [Tony Wiggins], but that's as close as we came to sharing."

EIGHT

AFTER ALMOST NINE MONTHS of nonstop touring the band elected to retire to the city of New Orleans for a semiworking vacation. Manson's growing cult in cyberspace was buzzing with news that a new single and video, "Dope Hat," were soon to be released, with an attendant headlining tour to support it. But as the band entered the studio to begin recording b-sides, the sessions began to stretch out, and it became apparent that something much more ambitious than a mere single was rearing its ugly head.

While fans waited with bated breath for news of the group's next release, there was still ample activity in the public eye to keep the masses entertained. Only a few weeks after the Danzig tour's conclusion, New York late-night television talk show host Jon Stewart decided to end his canceled series with a bang, not a whimper, and Manson were invited to perform as musical guests on his penultimate episode, taped on June 22, 1995. Living up to their outrageous reputation, the band took advantage of Stewart's no-lose situation, and concluded a two-song set of "Dope Hat" and "Lunchbox" by smashing their instruments and then torching the soundstage. Swept up in the merriment, Stewart's next guest, actor Cameron Bancroft, shattered his coffee mug on a table, slicing open his right palm, which began spurting very real blood. Backstage after the taping, paramedics wrapped up Bancroft while Mr. Manson shotgunned beers and Ginger did whippets, all under the watchful eye of *New York* magazine.

This was by no means the first time the band had caused a ruckus on television. Several months prior, Marilyn and Twiggy had appeared on *The Phil Donahue Show,* on an episode concerning the dangers of stage-diving, crowd surfing, and the mosh pit. The episode centered around the tragedy of eighteen-year-old Chris Mitchell, who'd died as a result of severe head injuries sustained after diving from the stage of a Life of Agony show in Brooklyn on December 17, 1994.

Even though talk show culture had inspired the birth of Marilyn Manson, the band and the man, the event proved anticlimactic for him. The audience didn't seem to know what to make of the rockers, who didn't come out until late in the show. "They didn't have any reaction," Manson told *The ROC.* "They didn't know whether to hate me or like me or be scared of me." By the time they formed an opinion, the show had wrapped up. "I think to be on there was appropriate, but I didn't think there was any way of actually getting my point across because people aren't really there to talk about the problem or try to solve the problem, they're only there to pick sides."

And as far as he was concerned, they weren't even addressing the right question. The subject shouldn't have been whether or not audiences should be allowed to mosh; the more important issue was how children and their folks related. "There needs to be a clear line of communication between parents, who may be informed about these things, and their kids, who may not," Manson later told *Family Circle* in a story on the same accident and the potential hazards at rock shows. "If parents trust their kids, and kids trust their parents, there won't be any confusion." But he also reiterated what should have been a very obvious point to anyone, regardless of age: "When it comes to stage diving, know that you're going to get hurt. We like to see our fans respond, but we don't like to see them hurt."

Or so the magazine claimed. Later, in an interview with Jon Pecorelli for *Alternative Press,* Manson remarked that he'd been misquoted as "a voice of reason." His comments on the Donahue show seemed to bear that out. "As far as stage-diving is concerned, my basic feelings are, if someone's stupid enough to jump off a stage, they can only expect to get hurt," he observed. "I think the same thing can probably go for a mosh pit; if you're gonna jump in there and start swimming around, expect to get hurt. I think a lot of people do and I think a lot of people are looking to get hurt, because it's also a pain rush that they're looking for. I don't know if there's any reasoning or deep philosophy behind why people mosh, but I think a lot of people want to get out that pain or want to receive that pain as part of being restricted, the same way that someone like me might be on any given day, and that's their outlet, and that's my outlet, and when we get together and the outlets click with each other, something more big and more powerful can come out of it."

Manson was frequently quizzed for his feelings concerning one of the season's most popular television events: the O. J. Simpson trial. "It's just another TV show, and a pretty boring one," he told *Rage*. "I'd like to think he's guilty, since we've already gone through all this hassle." And he could appreciate the impact of the negative publicity on the former football star's fame. "I think that one of the most ironic things about O. J. Simpson is that he was a star, and now his alleged crime has propelled him to be more infamous than he ever was as an actor," he said in *Livewire*. "It's kind of a backward scenario to the general twist of serial killers becoming popular."

Preoccupied with their recording schedule, the band proved just a mite too busy to return home for the 1995 Slammies, held on July 3 at the Edge in Fort Lauderdale. Marilyn Manson had been nominated for Band of the Year, Best Vocalist, Best National Release (for *POAAF*), and Best Single (for "Lunchbox"). They won the latter two, ironically beating out the Manson-produced "My Cat . . ." by Jack Off Jill for top single honors. The Slammie press release made a point of tersely noting that the band was busy filming a new video in New Orleans, "where they plan to relocate." But diehard fans of the South Florida scene didn't need to worry. While Marilyn Manson chose to record at Trent Reznor's Nothing Studio in New Orleans, and reside there sporadically throughout the next two years, they still maintained their Fort Lauderdale–area base of operations.

. . .

IF THE SUNNY CLIMES of Florida had played a vital role in the genesis of Marilyn Manson, the dark decadence of New Orleans was the perfect playground for what they had become. In the end, Manson even concluded that his exploits during their stay were rather cliché. He and Twiggy took to picking through graveyards on nighttime excavations. "I don't remember the names of the cemeteries we visited, but everywhere we went the ground was so eroded that we found bones just sticking out of the soil," he told *Tribe*. "You just kind of pick 'em like strawberries," he added in *High Times*. Twiggy in particular became fixated by this morbid pastime, and began accruing quite a collection to use as hair accessories, and took to carrying them with him on the road.

And apparently that wasn't all they were doing with bones. According to *Alternative Press*, the narcotics menu one night consisted of a hash of "Special K, crack, Tic Tacs and bits of human bone— in one pipe." The Mansons were partying in a hotel room with a bunch of strangers. "We talked them into chipping off pieces of the bones, putting it in a pipe and smoking it. We smoked it too. It was terrible—it smelled like burnt hair, gave you a really bad headache and made your eyes red."

Manson's account in *Tribe* of the mayhem on Twiggy's birthday was equally depraved. The boys ended up performing a tribute to their friend Tony Wiggins, the Danzig bus driver, a ritual that involved a one-legged black man Manson had become fascinated by, "an incredible amount of cocaine," and Jack Daniel's. "We ended up running around our neighborhood near Terpsichore at ten in the morning, completely naked, wearing wigs and cowboy hats. Twiggy had a lipstick swastika on his chest and was singing acoustic-guitar songs to a homeless guy named Joe, whom we gave a bottle of vodka." If the locals objected, Manson never heard about it. "I never met any of our neighbors, but I pissed on a couple of their porches," he claimed. "One time, I took a shit on a plate and left it in front of one of their doors."

"The only other time I spent at home was to sleep," said Manson.

"Twiggy and I called our bedroom the Crypt because it was an icy chamber with no decoration, no lighting, and a Salvation Army's worth of dirty clothes." In the end, they conceded that it was too simple to get sucked up in the excesses of New Orleans. "We did all the drugs there were to do, drank all the alcohol there was to drink, and dug up as many graves as possible." And amid the chaos and carnage, Manson and Twiggy had begun writing new songs for a projected second full-length album, scheduled to be recorded in early '96. The title, he revealed in the press, was *Antichrist Superstar*, and they envisioned it as "the sound track for the end of time."

IN THE MIDDLE OF the summer, Veronica Kirchoff got a phone call at her mother's house in Tacoma. It was Manson. He apologized for not keeping in touch, and gave her the lowdown on the band's new activities, and Sara Lee's departure. He mentioned that he'd been overwhelmed by how many fan letters and merchandise orders had piled up during their months on the road. Then all of the sudden, he asked if she was working. No, she was planning on going back to school in the fall, and wasn't doing much with her summer. "Do you want to run our fan club?" he asked.

Her reaction was "a mix of shock and flattery." He explained that they didn't have an official fan club, and that while she'd be paid for her work, she'd be starting from scratch: receiving, opening, and sorting fan mail, building a database, arranging special promotions for fan club members, who'd pay a small fee to join. She consented to do it, and Manson promised to talk to their new manager, Tony Ciulla, about setting everything up.

"He called me back a few days after that first time and hooked me up with numbers: to his parents' house in Florida, to the place in New Orleans where they were recording, [tour manager] Frankie's pager number, Tony's number at Nothing." An enormous box of unanswered mail was forwarded to her to get the ball rolling. And in the meantime, the singer wanted her to come down to New Orleans so they could discuss in person ideas for a newsletter, merchandise, and the best way to set up the fan club. She went down later that summer, for a three-or four-day spell. "I was down there to discuss business, and we didn't even get around to discussing anything remotely businesslike until the last day I was there, in the afternoon," she chuckles. Manson awoke and emerged from the Crypt. "He comes up in these baggy black boxer's sweat shorts, with a pad of paper and a pen, sits in a chair, and says, 'Okay, we need to talk about the fan club.' "

Veronica explained that she wanted the fan club to be a Marilyn Manson Family, and that members' dues would double as an adoption fee, for which they'd receive an official certificate. Manson, meanwhile, wanted the newsletter to resemble a church bulletin, right down to the tone, typeface, and layout. But the singer had trouble concentrating too long on the business at hand. "He had both feet up on the chair, and all he had on were his shorts." The two continued to brainstorm and Manson took notes. "And all of the sudden, he starts drawing little smiley faces on the bottom of his toes. Eyeball-eyeball-smile on each of his toes. Big, scary Marilyn Manson, drawing smiley faces on his feet. It was just so funny."

AS FALL ROLLED AROUND, the "Dope Hat" single had (d)evolved into *Smells Like Children*, a demented fifteen-track gumbo that was neither quite an LP nor an EP. In one especially painful interview, Manson told Joyce Marcel of InSiTe Features that the title was a nod to *Perfume*, a German book written by Patrick Susskind, then claimed the same text had inspired Kurt Cobain as well. "It's about a perfumer in the 1800s who smelled everything there was in the world," lied Manson. "And he found the most wonderful smell was the smell of innocent children."

In fact, *Smells Like Children* was another reference to one of Manson's favorite films and childhood bete noirs, the Child Catcher, the villain of the 1968 movie musical *Chitty Chitty Bang Bang*. "There was a character called the Child Catcher, he used his sense of smell to hunt down kids and kidnap them, and that was something that scared me when I was little," he reminded *huH* readers. "And when I got older, people reminded me of the character, they said, 'You really look like the Child Catcher'—I had become what I was afraid of." It was also the title of a song in progress slated for inclusion on *Antichrist Superstar*.

The theme of *Smells Like Children* was "use and abuse," an apt unifier considering everything going on sonically and socially during the recording. Manson also envisioned it as a contemporary children's record. "It was seeing everything from a child's point of view," he told Boyd Rice in *Seconds*. "It was grand and ugly at times. *Smells Like Children* is almost a metaphor for me trying to hold onto my childhood." And the title was a sarcastic swipe at critics who'd misread early Manson lyrics and interviews. "*Smells Like Children*, for me, was a bit of a joke because people always assume that things I mention in songs are promoting child molestation," he confessed to *huH*.

"Keep this and all drugs away from small children," announced the warning printed directly on the compact disc. Lord knows, there was so much depravity encoded on the disc that if tots had licked it, they probably would've hallucinated for hours. The fifteen tracks included eerie instrumentals ("The Hands of Small Children," "S★★★★y Chicken Gang Bang," Twiggy's "Scabs, Guns and Peanut Butter"), collages of samples from interviews and TV appearances ("Sympathy for the Parents," "Dancing with the One-Legged . . ."), and even a porn pastiche ("F★★k Frankie"). The meatier components were new and remixed versions of *POAAF* tracks ("Organ Grinder" became "Kiddie Grinder," "Everlasting C★★★sucker" was built from "Cake and Sodomy"), two renditions of "Dope Hat" ("Diary of a Dope Fiend" and "Dance of the Dope Hats"), and a country and western take on "Cake and Sodomy" ("White Trash"). But most interesting were the three covers (from which the original b-sides to the aborted "Dope Hat" single were to have been drawn); the Eurythmics' "Sweet Dreams (Are Made of This)," Screamin' Jay Hawkins's "I Put a Spell on You," and Patti Smith's "Rock 'n' Roll Nigger."

Much of the record was characterized by Manson's dark humor. The title "S★★★★y Chicken Gang Bang" was a both a nod to the Child Catcher and a less-than-subtle swipe at the chicken controversy dating back to the shows in Texas. Danzig's tour bus driver Tony Wiggins popped up on "White Trash (Remixed by Tony f. wiggins)." When a fan quizzed Manson on MTV OnLine as to the identities of the panting participants on "F★★★ Frankie," Manson replied, "They weren't all men, and they weren't necessarily Frankie either" (although the sleeve for *SLC* lists Frankie Proia as "Pornography Coordinator").

On a similar cyberspace chat for *SPIN*, the track came up again. "Marilyn, what was your mind going through when you made "F★★★ Frankie"? (Pogo is credited with composing the track).

"Am I going to get caught?" Manson shot back. "And how will I explain to the police all the blood and chicken feathers?"

Also fitting in with the whole abuse/use theme, "Dancing with the One-Legged . . ." was an obscure reference to the band's drug consumption. "We have this saying that when you are on certain types of drugs you are dancing with the one-legged man," Manson revealed to *Tribe*. "That man is the one-legged black man who's always hopping around by the interstate near St. Charles Avenue, begging money. I wanted to take his artificial leg." But later, he told his buddy (and fellow Church of Satan devotee) Boyd Rice a completely different story in *Seconds:* "I did have a Huggy Bear [from *Starsky & Hutch*] doll. One of his legs fell off. That empty leg became a place where, when we were doing a lot of drugs on tour at one point, we would store the drugs in his empty leg. That's where the term dancing with the one-legged man on *Smells Like Children* came from."

Perhaps the oddest track of all was "May Cause Discoloration of the Urine or Feces," which Manson claimed was built from a phone conversation he'd eavesdropped on. "I thought it would make a unique song that really dealt with other aspects of how drugs play into people's lives. This recorded conversation happens to be between two members of my family. These are the types of people who raised me, so I though that it might be an insight to share with others so they could see where I came from."

The record's high points were three of the band's best-loved cover versions: the Eurythmics' 1983 number one single "Sweet Dreams

(Are Made of This)," Screamin' Jay Hawkins's "I Put a Spell on You," and Patti Smith's "Rock 'n' Roll Nigger." Manson felt that all three were extremely powerful songs that hadn't been fully appreciated the first time around.

The choice of Screamin' Jay Hawkins's "I Put a Spell on You" seemed especially appropriate given all the hoopla surrounding Marilyn Manson. In 1956, Hawkins had a hit with his R & B voodoo tune. Although it seems timid by today's standards, forty years ago this Cleveland resident (what is in the Ohio water?) generated a tremendous amount of attention, and negative press, which claimed his rabid howling evoked anal rape and cannibalism. On stage, he played up the image, entering in a coffin and carrying a skull-topped scepter. Manson claimed the obsessive lyric was "the closest thing I could come to doing in a love song," and noted that its spooky vibe clicked with the New Orleans mentality.

Manson and Reznor had already discussed putting a cover of "Rock 'n' Roll Nigger" on the sound track of *Natural Born Killers* (Reznor had coordinated music for the film), but director Oliver Stone wanted the original version of the Patti Smith song from her 1978 album *Easter*. "It's a song that I remember hearing a long time ago and then hadn't heard for such a long time. And I thought it would be great to bring it to our generation, 'cause it's something they kind of missed out on. It's pretty much a perfect anthem for our audience," he told Gail Worley. "We are the ultimate minority, because people judge us by the way we look, and we are constantly fucked with because of it."

"Everybody gets pissed off when you say the word 'nigger,' " he added in *PM*. "The song is not a racist song. If anything . . . it's a song about being yourself and fuck everybody that doesn't try to understand that." As pop scholars Simon Reynolds and Joy Press point out in their book *The Sex Revolts*, Patti Smith had already invoked the freedom "to defy social order and break the slow kill monotony of censorship" in the sleeve notes for 1976's *Radio Ethiopia*. On the title track of *Easter*, "she imagines herself as a female Messiah resurrecting the spirit." Smith's title was already an homage itself, a nod to Yoko Ono's "Woman Is the Nigger of the World."

"If hipsters have always wanted to be White Negros, and woman is the nigger of the world, then why can't female rebellion be the model for all future rebels?" observe Reynolds and Press. Manson was simultaneously (as always) coming at the tune from opposite directions. On the one hand, he was a suburban white male with a background in metal, but on the other, he embraced the same ideas of blurred gender and sexuality that charged Smith's persona and work.

As for "Sweet Dreams," the band decided to give the new wave hit a much more somber treatment, one that would spotlight the lyrical themes of use and abuse. The repercussions of the tune (which had been in their set for quite some time) on the band's career would prove staggering, but not immediately.

Promotional copies of the finished disc were sent out in advance of the release date, but were recalled almost immediately, due to the inclusion of unlicensed samples from *Willy Wonka* and two hidden tracks, "Abuse Part 1 ('There Is Pain Involved')" and "Abuse Part 2 (Confession)." All the offending material had to be deleted, due to legal conflicts. Manson later told Gail Worley that the two "Abuse" cuts had "involved some illegal activities in the recording," and provoked a violent outburst from Tony Wiggins that only furthered the label's resolve to have them eliminated. But the back and forth delayed the record's release, and the band would end up going back out on tour before the product they were performing in support of became officially available.

And they finally made a video for "Dope Hat," which not surprisingly turned out to be a giddy and garish pastiche of the demented boat ride sequence from *Willy Wonka*. Stuffed with scantily clad babes, two dwarfs painted orange (to resemble Oompa-Loompas), a cameo from Dr. Anton LaVey, vicious scythes, and razor-trimmed lollipops, the clip was approved and rejected by MTV enough times to give the average fan a severe case of whiplash. The few times "Dope Hat" finally did air, in the less-than-prime-time hours between 2 and 5 A.M., it did so in an edited version.

Now the mainstream media were beginning to take serious note of the band. "Alice Cooper meets Sigue Sigue Sputnik, with all the shock-rock components: Boys in dresses, Frankenstein makeup, and weird-angle close-ups of dwarfs in fluorescent wigs suggest a sea cruise through Hades," noted *Entertainment Weekly.* "Underexposing keeps the images dark so Manson's death-pale face can dominate. His desperate sincerity is strangely touching, but the ornate production give the visual cliches more power than they deserve." They awarded the video a B grade.

But when *Smells Like Children* eventually hit the stores on October 24 (just in time for Halloween), the folks at *EW* were far less gracious. They dismissed *SLC* as an "artlessly assembled excuse for an album," and branded it with a D rating.

Nine

"SEE THEM BEFORE THEY are in jail, dead, or the biggest rock band in America!" announced the press release from Formula Public Relations, the small company whose hands had been kept quite full by the Manson family (as well as their flagship client, Nine Inch Nails) over the past year. And contrary to the predictions of assorted naysayers, the two-month "Smells Like Children" tour (which would eventually sprawl out to five months) would bring Marilyn Manson closer to the third choice on that list, despite their habitual flirtation with the first two.

The tour opened at Cain's Ballroom, in Tulsa, Oklahoma, on September 12, 1995. For those who chose to notice, the warm-up band was relatively unknown East/West recording artists Clutch. "He had a bug up his ass from the beginning," says Daisy Berkowitz of Manson's disposition, "because we had started the tour but the disc itself hadn't come out yet. He was like, 'I want it out when we're out!' " Berkowitz concurs that Manson's contention on this point is understandable, but the legal snafus surrounding "Abuse," parts 1 and 2, as well as the *Willy Wonka* samples, simply wouldn't permit *Smells Like Children* to come out on the original release date. That unfortunate set of circumstances didn't bode well for the rest of the outfit. "He'd built up some frustration and needed to take it out on whomever. But the disc came out in the middle of that tour."

The air of tension, plus the usual pressures of being on the road, meant that additional valves to release pressure were required. Daisy Berkowitz laughs when being reminded of dubbing the "Smells Like Children" jaunt "the Snow Tour." Because even though the five-month journey took the band through some of the most extreme and bone-chilling weather in U.S. history, that wasn't his primary inspiration for the nickname; the band's penchant for cocaine was. " 'The Snow Tour'? Yeah, you could call it that . . . if you know what I mean," he chuckles. "We were going skiing, but we didn't have any poles."

As a result of burdens of the elements and self-indulgence, Manson (who wasn't exactly the poster boy for respiratory health to begin with) "was ill with varying degrees of colds, flu, and bronchial pneumonia" for most of the trip, thus impeding his singing abilities. At several venues, he resorted to using oxygen hits from an offstage tank to get through the set.

But at the conclusion of the tour, Manson would freely admit to *High Times* what part of the problem was: he'd also started smoking marijuana regularly again, for the first time since high school. "When I started singing, I kind of stayed away from smoking because I thought it would hinder my throat." The bill of fare on the "Smells Like Children" tour had required a little something extra to even the mood out. "We were doing a lot of coke and crystal meth, stuff that pumps up the edge to my personality," Manson revealed. "I've never been one to want to take off the edge, but I guess out of boredom and wanting to try something new, I started smoking pot again."

Not that the rest of the band were blameless by any means. "Our keyboard player, Madonna, smokes pot from the minute he wakes up till the minute he goes to sleep," added the singer. "Both he and Daisy." (Manson, for the record, claimed he only referred to marijuana as "grass" or "reefer," never "pot.") And during the November 24 and 25 shows in Detroit, Twiggy managed to mistakenly consume a quantity of heroin, thinking the powdered white drug was something else. "I go out and cut 'em up, and think 'This tastes funny—is it speed or something?' It was horrible," he admitted in *Alternative Press*. "It was like I played in a coma."

Many of the hard-core Manson devotees apparently hated the opening act, Clutch, and made no secret of their displeasure. "Dull as wet cement, and Christian to boot, Clutch failed to endear themselves to Manson fans," Paula O'Keefe opined. But the Mansons themselves were fairly kind to the nondescript hard rock band in the press. "They're cool. I liked their first record a lot," Pogo told the *Gaston Gazette*. "They're great guys, I enjoy partying with them. . . . They're very different from us, which is good."

Part of what distinguished Clutch from Marilyn Manson was how seemingly ordinary they were in comparison. The contrast of outrageousness versus anonymity didn't sit well with some. But Manson raised some interesting points about the nature of T-shirt-and-jeans bands in *RIP*. "What people don't understand is with even the most politically correct bands out there, it's all a gimmick, it's all a lie. People may disregard Marilyn Manson as not being sincere because our imagery is so strong and the things I say are controversial, but the other bands who are playing it safe, that's their gimmick."

Perhaps more surprising, Clutch was equally supportive of Marilyn Manson. After a show in New York City on Friday, November 3, *The Village Voice* erroneously wrote: "It's no wonder that the anonymous warm-up band Clutch, whose members are Christians, refused to watch Manson and his crew." Clutch's manager, Jon Goldwater, quickly fired back a terse rejoinder: "If we took such offense at Manson, we would not be on tour with them. Quite the contrary, we have seen and enjoyed their performances on many occasions, and we have the utmost respect for what they do."

Meanwhile, Manson's violent stage behavior continued to claim nightly victims. "[Pogo] got hit in the head with a mike stand and it hit an artery and he almost bled to death," Manson claimed in the South Dakota rag *Tempest*. And at one of the Boston shows, on November 2, Manson smashed himself in the nose, yielding a pair of purple-black raccoon eyes the next day. "I did that myself though," he admitted to Gail Worley. "I hit myself with the microphone. . . . The microphone is a dangerous weapon in many ways, by the things that I say and the things that I do with it physically. Then a lot of people get harmed in different aspects by the microphone."

Manson handled a hilarious round of fan inquiries at the hands of *SPIN* OnLine. Although few of the questions asked were intended to do more than try and shock the rest of the audience, Mr. Manson parried them with abrasive charm. And clearly, the band were already thinking about their next album. One longtime fan asked "Any chance of 'Choklit Factory' or 'Negative 3' making it onto the *Antichrist* disc?" And Manson's answer came back, "No . . . but look for 'White Knuckles' & 'Suicide Snowman.' " But it was a rare foray into cyberspace, a domain of which Manson was already distrustful, despite the role of the Internet in bringing together his network on fans. "[I] just wanna . . . remind everyone that if you see my name on here that it isn't me, unless I appear on a legitimate format like this," he told an MTV OnLine assembly a few months later.

MEANWHILE, VERONICA KIRCHOFF HAD been cobbling together the Manson fan club, and creating a fresh newsletter to spread the word of the family. After visiting Christian bookstores and places of worship to get the tone and layout just right, she set to work, faxing ideas and content back and forth to Manson for input and approval. The original intention was that Veronica would write the majority of copy, with a special missive from Manson, à la a pastor's editorial. "But he never got around to it," she says. "Finally he went, 'Okay, I want you to write it, based on stuff that I've written before.' " On the one hand, she was irked. All she needed from him was a couple of paragraphs. "But then again, I was very flattered that he would allow me to write something coming from his mouth." And she appreciated that the band were tied up with recording *Smells Like Children* and touring.

Although she'd been in their employ for several months, Kirchoff didn't feel like her position was cemented until October, when the first newsletter was finally completed. Up till then, she'd been answering fan mail back with tour dates, and taking merchandise orders for Satan's Bakesale. But now, she had something physical to show the band and her peers. She sent out the first bulk mailing, to a total of five thousand addresses. "But we still had boxes and boxes of mail to go through," she admits.

Much to the chagrin of Kirchoff's post office box, her life became increasingly chaotic in a matter of a few weeks. But as newsletter responses began flowing in, her weekly merchandise orders swelled from $75 to $100 a week to upwards of $1,000. Combined with keeping track of all the incoming mail, and sifting through the contents to pluck out the items that Manson might find especially worthwhile, and keeping up the database, Kirchoff (who'd also returned to school in the fall) found herself increasingly busy.

And things only got worse when the second bulk mailing was sent out. Suddenly, the United States Postal Service came calling, with numerous concerns regarding the content of the newsletter. Apparently, a postal inspector had been upset to stumble across thousands of mailings for the Church of Antichrist Superstar. Kirchoff and her mother soon found themselves sitting down with a local postmaster, defending the p's and q's of their constitutional freedoms. Apparently, the USPS felt that Veronica had broken the law by using bulk mail to incite a riot. And once again. "They didn't like the KILL GOD / KILL YOUR MOM AND DAD / KILL YOURSELF shirt, because it was listed as KILL GOD / KILL YOUR MOM AND DAD / KILL YOURSELF [as opposed to the full shirt text]." She explained the full text in vain. The post office refused to budge, which in retrospect Kirchoff finds comical, "considering that the week before they had just sent a shipment of twice as many."

The list of offensive points seemed endless. The cover featured an antique woodcarving depicting *Walpurgisnacht* ("St. Walburga's night," when witches fly). It featured a picture of the devil on a throne, surrounded by dancing servants. In one corner of the image, some witches were tossing body parts into a kettle. "And the post office tried to say that that, combined with everything else in [the newsletter], was inciting people to cut other people up and boil them." Vulgar language was highlighted. "At the time it just pissed me off, but if I think about it objectively, it's funny what they were trying to construe as offensive." At one point, Kirchoff's mom even had to point out to the postmaster that *Chitty Chitty Bang Bang* was *not* a sexual reference.

All kidding aside, she was finding it much harder to pilot the fan club with the band now on the road. Getting in touch directly with Manson often took days. But finally, she tracked him down and shared with him an idea for getting back at the USPS. "I talked to Manson about it, I even talked to their tour manager about it," she remembers. "And they we all like, 'Yeah, go for it!' " So she made contact with the American Civil Liberties Union and scheduled an appointment. They sat her down with an attorney, who perused the newsletter and the documentation on both sides of the conflict. "He looked over it all, and they were really excited about it. 'Yeah, this is a great case.' Basically a precedent setter." But when Manson manager Tony Ciulla caught wind of the proceedings, Veronica claims he asked her to leave the matter alone for the time being; the band didn't need publicity like this.

And besides, she had plenty on her plate, filling orders and coordinating the bookkeeping for Satan's Bake Sale with the band's accountant in California. And when Christmas hit, her workload increased again, as Spooky Kids and neophytes alike shelled out their holiday dollars on Manson memorabilia. "We made three thousand dollars a week in merchandise orders." To compound matters, she elected to take a few days off to attend the New Year's Eve show in New York with two of her best friends, and fellow hardcore fans. "So I go away for five days, and come back, and there's three thousand dollars of orders waiting for me." She took a week off from school to try and catch up, but as the new orders kept coming in, the whole affair began to resemble a slapstick routine.

Adding fuel to the fire, there were some merchandise items that became difficult to keep in stock, and when the supplier ran out, she wasn't authorized to order a new run of T-shirts or stickers. Some things offered for sale never even seemed to exist in the first place. "I never, ever had a single poster, and I was told to keep that on the merchandise list." She'd call the supplier, only to be told they'd never made posters. Never mind that they were the only one legit merchandise supplier, and Veronica had seen Manson posters in stores.

"I ended up sending a lot of people credit vouchers, and saying, 'If you want your money back, let us know; if you want different merchandise, send this back and you can get it.' "

EVEN THOUGH TWIGGY ANNOUNCED in one interview that the band were no longer allowed to fraternize with bus driver Tony F. Wiggins, the "Southern gentleman" made an unexpected appearance at the December 4 Manson show at Jeremiah's, in Charlotte, North Carolina. But he didn't serenade the crowd with "White Trash." "He did a new composition called something like 'Can I Push in Your Stool,' described as a pickup line at gay bars," noted Paula O'Keefe. The band feted their old friend from start to finish: Manson had scrawled "Wiggins" across his torso, while Twiggy opted for "Tony" on his hand; the line "Tony Wiggins was a nigger" was substituted in "Rock 'n' Roll Nigger," and Manson even elected to slice several deep gashes into the guest of honor with a shattered beer bottle.

After a ten-day Christmas break following the December 17 show at the Edge, the tour resumed (with the Lunachicks opening), trying to capitalize on the momentum *Smells Like Children* (and especially "Sweet Dreams") was building. As the road stretched out further and further, tensions were coming to a head internally. One classic example occurred on the New Year's Eve show in New York at Roseland. "God, that was a night," recalls Daisy Berkowitz. "We had a big fight before sound check. I forget what it was about." The dynamic between the two original members was souring quickly. "I was getting frustrated, and started feeling cheated." And New York, a city Daisy loves, was the last place he wanted to feel undue pressure. "Any time you play New York or L.A., there's a million industry people there, backstage and watching the show. And I was really mad that this was going on, and he was getting his way, and I felt like shit . . . at that time, under those circumstances.

"I guess he was mad about the fight we had," says Daisy. Sure enough, at the gig's conclusion, Manson pushed the guitarist headlong into the crowd. After the show they had it out ("I threw a water bottle at him," he chortles), but no real peace was made. Being abused on stage, coupled with his increasingly diminished prominence in the band, was definitely beginning to wear on him. "There were a couple of times when he'd throw a mike stand at me, knock my gear over," Berkowitz reflects. "But that was the first night I seriously considered getting out of the band. Because I just couldn't take it anymore."

Daisy now claims his attempts to diffuse tension between the two original members were relatively fruitless. "There's a very vague memory in my head of talking to him, it might even have been on the tour bus, and saying, 'Listen, I feel like I'm getting excluded here . . . what's going on? I know you and Jeordie are working on stuff together, but I'm still here and I'm still important, and you should realize that.' " He sighs. "Maybe it doesn't stick in my head because the reaction I got was one of, 'Okay, I hear you,' but that's it. No promises. He didn't say anything that made me feel better, just something to placate me."

According to the reports from John Pecorelli of *Alternative Press*, who tagged along with the quintet for the rest of the holiday mayhem, things only got weirder as that New Year's Eve unfurled into morning. The band managed to navigate their way from the Academy Theater through the party-hearty Times Square crowd, and piled into a van headed for a fete hosted by MTV Veejay and beloved Republican spokesmodel Kennedy. "It's clear Marilyn's not comfortable," assessed Pecorelli of the singer's reaction to the room filled with music industry players and other performers. At one point, Mr. Manson singled out the reputedly antisocial J Mascis of Dinosaur Jr., whispering, "We should kill him." When another reveler offered Marilyn a hit of ecstasy, he smiled and declined. "Sorry, you've got the wrong guy." Meanwhile, Daisy (who the author noted looked "almost conservative by Manson standards in green hair and peacoat") seemed to be reeling from the less-than-delightful effects of mixing hash, booze, and ecstasy. In another room, Pogo was busy detailing surefire ways to commit suicide with various munitions.

Among the most hilarious anecdotes in the Manson annals took place in Allentown, Pennsylvania, following the quintet's January 6 show at the club Starz. That weekend, "Blizzard '96" struck, dumping several feet of snow all up and down the eastern seaboard. The city of Philadelphia closed up shop, and Pennsylvania ground to a halt. Thus a hotel in the industrial town of Allentown ended up providing shelter and sustenance to not only Marilyn Manson, but also a rerouted Orlando Magic, the basketball team featuring seven-foot superstar Shaquille O'Neal (himself a recording artist), and a bus and truck company of *Sesame Street Live*.

"Remember the bar scene from *Star Wars* with all the animals?" explained Magic backup center Jon Koncak to the *New York Times*. "That's what it looked like last night. It was the *Twilight Zone*, man. A bunch of basketball players, *Sesame Street*, and some guy with green hair dressed like the Grim Reaper, chain-smoking. You needed a video camera to believe it. I'm still trying to deal with it."

O'Neal and the other players purportedly went out of their way to make introductions to members of both camps seeking refuge in Trophy's, the hotel bar. Koncak felt the experience was especially rewarding for Shaq, "because once they got over who he was and that we were all stuck there together, it was no big deal." It seems unlikely that Manson, Twiggy, and crew would've been clamoring for autographs (or trying to convince him to do a cameo rap on their next LP) in the first place. And the Magic took note of that. After erroneously referring to the Mansons as "those Nine Inch Nails guys," Koncak noted that "if one looks over at you more than three times, you just know your time is up."

The inclement weather necessitated the cancellation of the band's next two shows, but by January 10 the show was up and running again, at least for a while. But then, between January 23 and January 30, a string of dates in the South had to be canceled. No doubt the ascension of the band's profile was only placing increasing amounts of pressure on all parties involved, particularly their leader. "That's when things were getting technically bigger," confirms Daisy. "He wanted more lights, and 'Sweet Dreams' was getting a lot of exposure and really pushing us up. He started taking things a lot more seriously, because we started doing well."

The rise in attention had other repercussions, too. "I'm sure at that point, he decided to be more strict about everything," adds Berkowitz, who found himself on Manson's bad side more and more often. "He'd always complain about my clothes and my makeup: 'You look like shit.' " Berkowitz told Manson to purchase him new clothes if he didn't like his garb, but the singer wouldn't, and told him to shell out for them out of his own pocket. "And he would have his Nothing credit card to get whatever he wanted. He could've bought anything for the whole band, at any time. But he bought rings and clothes and shoes and stylist appointments, for himself."

After pulling off the final dates in Florida, the tour finally ground to a halt on February 4, at the Playground in Stuart, Florida. Remarkably, the band had made it through their most grueling stint on the road to date with a minimum of mishaps. "It was always reasonably under control," says Daisy. "We had pretty good management on the road. There is nothing I can think of that got really out of hand, where anybody got arrested or hurt . . . just the usual rock and roll craziness."

TEN

NIGHT AFTER NIGHT MORE and more audience members in attendance at "Smells Like Children" dates were waiting to hear the same specific song: "Sweet Dreams (Are Made of This)." Manson's version of the Eurythmics smash emphasized the "abuse" aspect of the song a lot more blatantly than the original. "A lot of people hadn't gotten that element out of it," Manson noted of the song to *Jam*. Manson's detractors had laughed when he first started doing the number, but he genuinely felt there was a powerful message buried in the words. "I identified so much with the way that it looks at relationships, and I wanted to focus on the lyrics."

"Also, after our first record, which so many people thought was bombastic and offensive, I thought one of the more shocking things I could do was cover a Eurythmics song," he added in *Billboard*.

The selection actually fit into Manson's overall musical aesthetic. When *Guitar World* asked Manson to list his influences, he had mentioned Adam Ant, David Bowie, Annie Lennox, and Bauhaus, in addition to his usual litany of shock metal superstars. "One of my favorite records is *Mob Rules*, when Dio sang for Black Sabbath," he added. "I even like Creedence Clearwater Revival. I like dark things; not only predictable dark things, but things that you might not expect to have a lot of pain in them, but do." And Dave Stewart, the composer of "Sweet Dreams," certainly wasn't complaining. "I heard from other people that he liked it a lot. I'm sure he's happy because he made a lot of money off of it, and we didn't."

Indeed, "Sweet Dreams" was making greater inroads for Marilyn Manson than anything they'd done to date. By spring, the video for the track had been labeled a Buzz clip by MTV, while the song was already in rotation on over fifty modern rock stations nationwide. In the first six months of release, *Smells Like Children* sold over 190,000 copies. In the last week of April, it jumped from the No. 115 spot on the *Billboard* 200 to No. 60.

The role of MTV in the track's success was the source of much conflict. In the past, the network had only given Manson videos the most marginal airtime. And the band seemed to accept that, having already rejected the network as "too safe." They were building their reputation largely by staying on the road giving dynamite shows, and weren't about to seriously modify their act for the mainstream. "It's really hard to decide what MTV likes," Manson had mentioned to *Circus* when the "Dope Hat" video fell on stony ground. "I just like to make a video, and if I'm happy with it then that's all that really counts."

Up to now, MTV hadn't felt comfortable with an act as dark and confrontational as Marilyn Manson. But the success of bands like Filter, Stabbing Westward, and Gravity Kills was changing that. "Often, there are a lot of bands that do a more commercial version of what bands like us or Nine Inch Nails do, and it kind of opens the doors for the bands who have been around longer doing the same thing but don't do it commercially," Manson noted in *Billboard*. "Often, the people who imitate what you do make it possible for you to be successful, much like Stone Temple Pilots did for Pearl Jam in another category."

MANY OF THE LONG-TERM fans were less than pleased that the band had achieved mainstream triumph, especially considering the song with which they'd done so. "That was really a problem," recalls Paula

O'Keefe. On-line, the battle raged between dissenting groups of Manson followers. "There were so many people who felt that it was a blatant ploy for popularity, for mass popularity, and that it would attract the wrong kind of people."

O'Keefe understands why the original fans were so defensive. "One of the things about Manson fans, at least at that time, is that they're very insular. We very much felt like we were a family, a community, a tight little group of freaks. And that letting in all these people who did not get it would destroy everything. There was much manning of the barricades and pulling up the drawbridge when that song came out. Especially when it became—gasp, horror—a Buzz clip. The discussion on that went on for weeks and weeks."

Regardless of where they were coming from, the new fans, who ranged from "the newly devoted to the merely curious and the thoughtlessly trendy," didn't fit in well with the older fans, the self-appointed Spooky Kids. The neophytes were dubbed Sweet Dreamers, and reviled by many, and understandably so, O'Keefe contends. "The core of Marilyn Manson fandom is hurt and troubled kids to whom MM's music and ideas are intensely personal."

In the end, the dust soon settled, and the Spooky Kids learned what many music industry insiders already realized: Often, the MTV generation is only loyal to a band for the length of one record, or even a single song, and then it moves on to the next Buzz band. "It's a funny thing," O'Keefe agrees. "People are very alarmist, but things simmer down. It was kind of shocking for a while to find all these kids you were sure had never heard of them wearing their Manson shirts at the mall. But that doesn't make them idiots. A lot of the [older] fans are very judgmental, and possessive. People can be just as earnest fans if they're newcomers."

Manson was fully aware that much of his adoring public was displeased with the success of the single. "But to me it was just a clever piece of cheese on a rat trap!" he pointed out to *Alternative Press*. "A lot of innocuous mall shoppers bought 'Sweet Dreams' and were then introduced to this whole new world of Marilyn Manson that they didn't expect. And ultimately that's the most devious thing you could ever pull off, and I don't think some of our fans appreciate the irony of that.

"I've never done anything that I felt compromised what the band was about in order to succeed—I feel like I've always utilized what the band was about in order to succeed." And contrary to some accusations, money was not the motivation. "This band has always been about pulling one over on the mainstream, about being a real-life joy buzzer or whoopee cushion, just to fuck with things because they need to be fucked with." True fans, he reasoned, would divine and understand this principle.

And besides, it wasn't necessarily the majority of fans, just a cadre of diehards. "But if they really believe in it, they should be out on the street corner playing the album for people." If music and society were going to change, Marilyn Manson and their followers had to yell it from the top of the highest hill. "In that sense it's not unlike Christianity. I remember hearing the same thing when I was a kid, that I should be out witnessing to other people. And it is the same. The only way that we're going to make a change is if we fight fire with fire."

And as even their fame swelled, the band's convictions were there for the world to see. "I want everyone to know that this recent success can only make what we stand for stronger and that I will never sell out what I stand for," Manson declared on MTV OnLine on April 29, 1996. "Everyone stay tuned for *Antichrist Superstar*." And no matter how many copies of "Sweet Dreams" were flying out of the stores, the new album (which the band had begun recording in February) was definitely the priority. The success of "Sweet Dreams" was just the herald of something much greater, Manson portended in *Billboard*. "Obviously, music and attitudes change with the times, and as we get closer and closer to destruction, it's getting more interesting, because we're becoming more and more desensitized."

"SWEET DREAMS" HAD A severe impact on the fan club, too. "It stopped being fun real fast," pronounces Veronica flatly. No matter how many orders came in, she was still earning a flat one hundred dollars a week, even when she put in a sixty-hour week. "Manson kept saying that I was going to be well taken care of. Because around this time the 'Sweet Dreams' video was out, and they were doing really good. It started to take off, and they're starting to really see some income from it." There was talk of paying her a bigger salary, or handing over all the merchandise responsibilities, so she could concentrate exclusively on the fan club, or hiring an assistant.

But Veronica's discussions with Manson only served to placate her; results were not forthcoming. "Every time I talked to him, he would tell me all this stuff." He would promise to bring her grievances to management, or the label. "And whether he ever talked to anybody about it or not, I don't know. I don't know if he talked to people and they put it off, or if he was putting it off. I'd like to think that he was keeping his side of the deal and letting people know it was too much for me.

"I started really losing interest, and losing faith in Manson, as a friend, because nothing was being done. And every time I talked to him, it almost always started off with me saying, 'I quit, I can't do this anymore, I'm sending all this shit back.' But then by the end of the conversation he'd talk me back into it." Tony Ciulla, on the other hand, was much more impersonal, even after she finally met him during the visit to New York for the New Year. "He was cool with me, but he's a businessman."

Things finally came to a head as the "Smells Like Children" tour was winding down and "Sweet Dreams" was taking off. She was sitting at her desk at the school newspaper where she worked, opening merchandise sales. "In one day I had nine hundred and fifty dollars in orders." She started laughing maniacally, and a colleague who knew the score leaned over and asked what was up

"I have nine hundred fifty dollars' worth of orders!" announced Veronica.

"Since when?"

"Since today!"

"I hope you're getting a percentage," her pal replied. A lightbulb went off over Veronica's head. She decided to give them an ultimatum, and ask for a share of the profits. If it was a slow week, she'd earn less, but she'd also have less to do. And when things were crazy, she'd have profits as an incentive. "So I talked to Manson shortly thereafter, and he says, 'Yeah, that's fine, that sounds reasonable.' " But once again, the situation seemed to culminate in promises that didn't lead to action. Finally, she announced that she wanted to be paid either ten dollars an hour, or 10 to 15 percent of the merchandise profits. Still no definite answers were forthcoming. So she decided that in exchange for her one hundred dollars per week, she'd do ten hours of work, or fill a thousand dollars' worth of orders, "and that's all." Until a resolution was reached, the mailing list would have to wait, and if orders backed up, so be it.

THE SUCCESS OF "SWEET Dreams" also brought Manson to the attention of another audience. Rusty Benson, associate editor of the *AFA Journal*, a bulletin published by the Reverend Donald Wildmon's American Family Association, first learned of the band during their initial flush of mainstream fame. "Marilyn Manson first caught my attention one day when I was at home eating lunch and channel surfing," Benson writes. "I caught the 'Sweet Dreams' video on MTV. Although I'm not easily bothered by music videos, I admit that this video got my attention, because of its extremely disturbing images. My interest was piqued when I learned that the video had broken into MTV's Top 20 videos. This seemed remarkable since the Top 20 generally reflects 'mainline' tastes. I was aware of such acts, but none this extreme had broken into the mainstream. Our first news stories were written from this perspective.

"I began to research the band and learned of their blatant anti-Christian sentiments," he continues. "This, of course, piqued my interest."

Sure enough, within two months, the *AFA Journal* had addressed the topic of Marilyn Manson, in an article entitled "Satanic Death-Rock Band Goes Mainstream." Aside from the misleading billing "death-rock," the contents of the story simply recounted the facts as they saw them (culled primarily from reputable music magazines), although it noted that the hit currently bringing them wide attention was "tame compared to most of its profanity laden tunes."

"The video for 'Sweet Dreams (Are Made of This)', however, is a different story. The picture clip, complete with subtle references to the Church of Satan, has worked its way onto Music Television's (MTV) heavy rotation list and onto the music channel's Top Twenty countdown." Benson echoed Manson's motivation almost word for word. "It's a classic case of bait and switch. Draw teen listeners in with a commercial hit and then expose them to the darker side of the music and the message." The *AFA Journal*'s monthly subscribers, some four hundred thousand strong, were now on the alert.

ELEVEN

EVEN AS "SWEET DREAMS" was exploding nationally, the band was squirreled away at Reznor's Nothing Studios, on Magazine Street near Audubon Park, working on the new album. Although the decision to return to New Orleans was influenced in part by financial and technical concerns, the locale's appeal and its influence on the band were undeniable. "If I had to pick any place in America that was Earth's equivalent of Hell, it would be New Orleans, because I think it's a place where people come to die," said Manson of their decision to return, in an interview with Paul Semel for *huH*. "There's a saying here in New Orleans, 'There's two things here: bars and graveyards.' " Manson couldn't deny that despair and misery seemed to permeate the surroundings. "But at the same time you can use that to your advantage. You can see how worthwhile life is by being so near the ugliness of it all. And, luckily, that's what I managed to do.

"It's a real dark town, and that's not to try and play up any sort of hype for New Orleans, it's just a really ugly place. It's something you don't see when you're just here for a day or two, but when you're here for months it really works at you."

Antichrist Superstar was ostensibly going to be the sound track for the end of time, the record that would bring about the apocalypse.

Needless to say, all parties involved wanted to get it right. Reznor's involvement on *Antichrist Superstar* was even greater than on the past two Marilyn Manson records. "That was something we wanted," Manson told *Guitar World*. Manson and Twiggy had written the bulk of the material—with additional contributions from Pogo and Daisy—largely over the past two years (although some material dated as far back as *POAAF* and earlier). "But we wanted to go to an outside source like Trent and have him put our vision together, because we were just too close to it." Other producers, including Bob Ezrin, were considered for the task, but ultimately Trent seemed like the wisest choice. "We decided that, since he knew us best and we get along together, that it was best to go along with him."

While the bulk of *POAAF* had sprung from the creative team of Manson and Berkowitz, the singer had invested the majority of time for *Antichrist* writing with Twiggy, taking advantage of their symbiotic friendship and using that connection as a conduit for his convoluted aesthetic. "I'm a little too close to it now to step back and look at that," he told *Guitar School* later, "but when Twiggy and I were writing the record, I would come to him with these dreams that I had, lyrically, and we would understand each other, and the music would come from the same place." In the past, they had written more as a democratic unit, with each player supplying his own parts. *Antichrist Superstar* was different. "But this was very focused and it came from a specific place in our minds and he and I specifically were in tune with one another. And Pogo, for that matter, also." That core trio had written the bulk of the material. And as Manson noted, in numerology, "there's a lot of significance to the number three. It's traditionally a very powerful number, you find it in a lot of religions, and there's a reason for that. It's the holy trinity, in magic it's a very powerful number."

Even though he didn't write any songs per se, new drummer Ginger Fish's electronic background paid off when the Manson family commenced work on *Antichrist Superstar*. Even out of the "Smells Like Children" tour, he'd pitched in during offstage time. "Obviously, you spend a lot of time on the bus and in the hotel," Fish said in *Drum* magazine. "So a lot of the songs were written on drum machines sitting in the room with Manson and Twiggy, the bass player who played guitar on most of the album, too. The three of us would sit in a room all day saying, 'Okay, let's try something with this drumbeat, this bass riff.' "

In the end, a large percentage of the preproduction for the album was done on the road. When the group finally settled into the studio, Ginger downloaded his drum machine parts into Reznor's array of computers. The rhythmic structures of *Antichrist Superstar* were then tampered with extensively, augmented and diminished, elongated and contracted, until a verdict between all the vital players had been reached. Only then would Fish actually tackle pounding the skins. The drum machine tracks would be muted, and he'd play in synch with a click track. "In the final mix, there were some songs where I played verses and the drum machine played the choruses, or vice versa. On some songs I'm playing totally live or played two passes: one on the snare and bass drum, and then I played toms on another or played into Protools [software]. We cut and spliced everything."

Meanwhile, engineer and coproducer Dave Ogilvie (of Skinny Puppy fame) dedicated himself to exploring every dark corner of the Reznor homestead in search of spots that would be conducive to experimental recording. "He did a lot of different miking techniques in different rooms of the studio for each song," Fish explained to *Drum*. One track was even recorded in the garage. "Dave actually miked Trent's Porsche. He opened the doors up and used them as a reflecting wall. We did it to sort of cure some boredom at the time, but it ended up working and it sounded really good." But at the end of the day, two people were calling the shots. "Obviously, Trent came in and had the final word on it, and Manson was there for every bit. Manson's always around for everything."

The band's previous album had been nourished on a diet of talk shows, classic children's television, and junk food. But *Antichrist Superstar* was a much more ambitious undertaking altogether. From start to finish, experimentation was the order of the day. "We experimented in pain, experimented in narcotics, Hebrew cabalism, numerology has become very important on the new album—when you look at it very carefully people can read into a lot of the numbers and the symbols." Manson told *huH*.

"All of this stuff is timeless, in that a lot of it was culled from dreams that I've been having," Manson struggled to explain in *CMJ New Music Monthly*. In Manson's opinion, the past and the future had begun to dovetail right before his eyes. "I've learned to approach my life like an old fashioned movie camera, in that all of the frames are contained in the camera, all of the pictures are there. You're only allowed to see one at a time, but I've kind of opened it up and looked at all of them, and that's what this record is."

Thus the chronology of the album's genesis tended to elude him in interviews. He told *huH* he couldn't pinpoint writing an individual song or lyric, or even the specific inspiration behind them necessarily, after the album was completed. "There are songs on the album that are innately written from my point of view, and there are some that are from some personality that I don't understand, that I've decided to label Antichrist Superstar," he claimed. "Just because I'm done with the album, doesn't mean I understand it any more than anyone else who's going to listen to it."

In some regards, Manson felt as though he were "in a movie that I write as I go along." The record spoke of events that hadn't happened yet, and addressed issues of a popularity that the band hadn't yet achieved. "Over the past year, I've kept a diary of what I was dreaming, almost like John the Baptist's visions of things to come," he said. "In the studio, we'd go about different ways to enhance that. We brought out our subconscious when making this record."

"I don't know if I really dreamed those songs, or if those songs dreamed me, or if they were something from the future or something I wrote a long time ago," Manson confided to Semel. "There's no real clear definition between what has happened and what will happen when you open your mind and you let yourself be on a different level of . . . awareness."

"That's why a lot of people, when they've been through severe traumas and they feel like they've talked to God or they've been abducted by aliens it's because they've come in touch with that same experience, but they didn't actually grasp on to it," Manson suggested to *Guitar World*.

"Stay up for a week, it'll change your life," giggled Twiggy. "We had contests to see who could stay up the longest."

They also spent a fair amount of time in the studio just staring at one another, trying to tap into a psychic vibe that didn't require words. "Twiggy and I have a system where, a lot of times, I don't have to tell him what I'm thinking; he just knows." But one thing was certain. Tapping into the subconscious doesn't happen by sitting around and consciously willing oneself to unlock those doors in the psyche. Hence the extensive forays into narcotic use, self-inflicted pain, and sleep deprivation. "I had this impression that this was going to be easy," Twiggy said with a shrug for *Seconds*. "I thought I was just going to glide through and it ended up being one of the hardest things I've ever done." In the end, it proved mentally and spiritually taxing, not to mention physically demanding. But every ounce of effort would be audible on the finished product.

Manson also looked at the myths of Antichrist figures from a variety of cultures. "I like the idea of the legend of the watchtowers for the end of the world that can only be released by mankind," he admitted to *Seconds*. Frequent mention was made of the Kabbalah, an ancient Jewish system of mysticism. Meanwhile Pogo, who'd dabbled with various philosophies even before joining the band, delved into numerology, and was very specific about the correlation between the sounds and frequencies he selected. "I don't have a complete understanding of what he did but we made it all tie together tightly," the singer admitted. "Anything that seems deliberate is, and anything that seems random is also deliberate."

"I'm a person that watches everything," Manson reminded *Guitar World*. In public, he observed people; in private, he listened to his own dreams. "I listen to voices on cellular phones that I'm not supposed to be hearing. I listen to conversations that people have. I'm just in tune with everything. When you get to that level, where every frequency is audible to you, then you find everything really ties together. It can be scary for some people, but if you're a part of it, it's kind of exciting."

In countless interviews, Manson insisted that he'd become accustomed to being attuned to so much activity on so many psychic levels. "I also pay close attention to déjà vu," he added in *Seconds*. "I haven't finished my theory on it, but I feel we will develop the ability to send messages to ourselves in the future. That's what I think déjà vu is. Psychologists have a name for a disorder called 'the delusional self' and that's when you think everything's related for a reason, but I think there are higher forms of awareness."

"Listen, let me just tell you something," announces Daisy Berkowitz when asked to reflect on Manson's unconventional approach to composing *Antichrist Superstar*. "For press reasons, of course, he'll say 'experiments dealing with sleep deprivation.' That comes from that thing, what is it called . . . oh, cocaine! That's 'sleep deprivation.' Just bullshit like that, and partying a lot, because Trent's that way and there he is in his own studio, he's not paying the bills, and it's New Orleans. If you've ever been in New Orleans, you know it's a great, wonderful city, but don't plan on holding on to your money or your sanity. So they would get real irresponsible sometimes. A lot of what was in the press regarding that kind of behavior was kind of candy-coating it somewhat, or saying it in a different way to make it seem more mysterious.

"And anything Manson knows of the Kabbalah," he continues, "Pogo informed him of. Because I don't think he would've thought about it twice. Unless Anton LaVey told him to. [LaVey's] a great guy, but he's really just an old carny. A lot of people his age leave their houses."

CLEARLY, AS *ANTICHRIST SUPERSTAR* took shape, Berkowitz and Manson were seeing eye to eye less than ever before. Throughout the "Smells Like Children" tour, Berkowitz had been aware that Twiggy and Manson were working on new material. "But I didn't think it would be dwindled down to most of the material coming from just them," he adds. And while he suspected that his involvement in the creative process for the new album wasn't going to be nearly as significant as in the past, he thought he'd be involved to a greater extent than he ultimately was.

Berkowitz claims that during the band's first stay in New Orleans, after the tour with Danzig and during the making of *Smells Like Children*, he had begun writing for the next album, along with the rest of the band. "We had about five or seven songs that we put together as a group. Some of them being 'Antichrist Superstar' and 'Irresponsible Hate Anthem.' [The music for] 'Hate Anthem' I wrote on my own, and everyone else put their two cents in . . . but [it was] mainly written by me." (*Antichrist Superstar* credits the music to Berkowitz and Gacy, lyrics to Manson and Ramirez.)

"Then there were songs like 'Antichrist Superstar,' which we all collaborated on," he continues. "And there was the tape that I had made with about a dozen songs that I came up with on my own, that I gave to Brian to listen to. And he only picked one of them, which turned out to be 'Wormboy.' And I also had an intro that he really liked, but when it became time to record songs for *Antichrist* . . . , it had been scratched by him and Trent." Daisy also confirms that "Suicide Snowman," which had been in the set for roughly two years, was originally in the running. "That [song] has always been a favorite of our longest-running fans. But that was scratched, too. He felt it didn't fit in with the concept of the record."

Likewise, his contributions in the studio amounted to "not much at all. Since a bunch of the songs were put together by Brian and Jeordie, and Jeordie also plays guitar, so he played guitar on those. They were there four days a week or so, and I was only in one or two, to focus on the songs that I came up with, or I started." An us-versus-them mentality began to settle over his disposition. "I knew that them being down there every day, and me being down every couple of days, was not a good sign."

Finally, near the end of the spring, the hammer fell. "I'd had a long talk with Frankie Proia, who was our road manager, in my hotel room in New Orleans, while working on *Antichrist Superstar*," Daisy recounts. "And he made me realize a whole bunch of things, and I had it in my head to quit. 'You're right, what am I doing?' And I called up [manager] Tony Ciulla in New York, and said, 'Tell Brian we need to talk, because I can't take this anymore.'"

The whole band convened for a meeting, and Daisy aired his grievances. "I said, 'I can't take this anymore if I'm not going to get any respect, or any credit for anything. I'm out. This is ridiculous, you're being totally unfair.' And nobody—Trent, Trent's partner, Brian, nobody in the band—said, 'Well, hold on, maybe that's a rash decision, maybe we can work something out.' Nobody said anything to that effect. As soon as I got home, I realized that. And I said, 'Well, I did do the right thing, because these people do not fuckin' care.' Every once in a while I think, 'Maybe I should've stayed in, they got all big after I left,' but when I think about that, it's like, 'No.' Maybe I should've left even sooner."

Once the album was finished, Manson would speak frequently in the press about Berkowitz's departure. "There's always been an element of friction there—one of those singer/guitar player tension things," he told *Guitar World*, noting that their relationship had grown increasingly turbulent during the *SLC* tour. "But in our case, it never really jelled into a good working dynamic." Daisy, he insisted, was more concerned with his own singular style than the greater good of the song or album they were working on. "I'm always looking at the bigger picture. Sometimes his vision was a little narrower."

Manson also confirmed that Berkowitz's participation in the writing and recording of the new record had been minimal. "We wanted to approach this record in a much more experimental, open-minded way. I wanted to play guitar. Twiggy wanted to play guitar. We wanted to go into it like the [Beatles'] *White Album*. These songs come from places that the songs on the first record didn't come from." The role Berkowitz had played in the creation of earlier material didn't fit into that scheme. And as Daisy had already said, he thought most of Manson's "experiments" were bogus pursuits. "He wasn't into making life into art. He looked at it more as a job, whereas we embraced life and art as one." But then he added, "It wasn't a nasty decision for him to leave."

"I've found that the most important criteria for anyone, and I realized this just this last year, is that if they don't believe in what I believe in, it's just not gonna work," Manson declared in *CMJ New Music Monthly*. "And I had to say to myself, starting this record, 'If I believe half the things I'm trying to say, then I need to make a change.' " And one of the specific changes required was dealing with Daisy, whom he didn't feel took the deeper ideas behind the band and their music seriously. "[That] was always very soul destroying for me. I think there was always a bit of insecurity on my part; he and I had written the music together, so there was a fear of how much the band would change. But I found in starting this album that the thing that I feared losing was the thing that was really limiting us from being the thing that we were going to be." When Berkowitz left, "it was trimming away the last piece of fat that was holding us back from being as strong as possible. Not to say that his work with us wasn't good, but it was something that Marilyn Manson had grown out of."

And though the split sounds reasonably professional, Manson finally revealed how deep his frustrations truly ran. "I don't know if he'll ever realize how much it didn't work, because I had a great amount of animosity for many years, and he never really managed to realize it. And I thought I was really apparent about it." Like on New Year's Eve, for example. But with that cumbersome tie to the past severed, Manson felt much of his anger subsiding. "Twiggy and I, and Pogo for that matter, really put our hearts into this record, and it means a lot to us. There's always gonna be Marilyn Manson the band, but the three of us is the core behind the belief system in the band."

"I appreciate the fans in a way I don't think he could," Manson later claimed in *Alternative Press* when a fan chided him for dismissing Daisy's departure on MTV's *120 Minutes*. "I feel as though they're a part of me; I don't look at them as people who I have to sign autographs for, or that I'm making money off of. I'm not sure if he saw it the same way. But that's just my perception; I may be wrong." But that's one accusation the guitarist refuses to take lightly. "I've always treated fans with the utmost respect, because they are the kids that buy the tickets and the records and the T-shirts, and they deserve respect. I've always treated them with as much respect as I could, even if I felt shitty or didn't want to talk to any of them. Brian and Jeordie will . . . they'll be nice and sign autographs, but they were the ones most likely to treat people like shit if they were in a mood."

Daisy returned to his home base in Florida and slowly began to cobble together a post–Marilyn Manson life. He resumed using the name Scott Mitchell, and eventually announced the formation of his new band, Three-Ton Gate, featuring singer Tyreah James. "Ultimately, what I'd like to do is be in a situation where I can just sit in the studio and work on music for sound tracks, and produce other bands." The future, he insists, looks very promising. "There are fans out there that are very eager to hear my new stuff, and that's a really good feeling."

THE AUDITION PROCESS TO recruit a replacement began in May, with a classified advertisement seeking a new lead guitarist for the band placed in a variety of urban weeklies. Tony Ciulla contacted candidates about six weeks later, informing the lucky applicants that only a small number of potential talents had been selected to audition from a pool of a thousand-odd axmen who'd submitted the requisite tape, photo, and bio to a New Orleans address. As Brian B. Wilson detailed in "Beautiful Losers," his *Guitar World* feature concerning two such subjects, the nominees concentrated on figuring out the best way to fill Daisy's big shoes before heading out for auditions in mid-July. The actual tryouts were held at the Nothing Studios. In the waiting room, candidates filled out questionnaires that included inquiries such as:

"1. What is your symbol of personal power?
2. How do you feel about people of color?
3. What is your definition of art?
4. If you had sex with a man but were not in love with him, does that mean you are gay? Explain."

Among the other candidates that afternoon was a slight young man from Chicago named Michael Timothy Linton, who'd played briefly with Life, Sex and Death. "I never actually played in a band that actually did any recording," he later told *Guitar World*. He had jammed with local musicians, but mostly stuck to making recordings at home. For his demo submission, he had selected three or four songs out of a back catalog of roughly seventy four-tracks. Linton had also been fortunate enough to have seen the band at the Metro once before, and knew the material from the other two records fairly well.

Approximately fifteen potential new members (in *Seconds* Manson says they received about "a million tapes," but invited less than twenty people to try out) shuffled around the waiting room, watching as the competition entered the audition studio, one by one. "It was your typical mix: You had an alternative crowd; five or six Twiggys in the room; a couple of goth guys. I had no idea where I would fit in. I wore a T-shirt and black jeans."

When the time finally came for individuals to show off their goods, they were ushered into a darkened audition room. All they could see was a Marshall stack and a glaring spotlight directed upon it. Because of time constraints, some candidates were prohibited from using effects units. Manson listened on the couch, with Twiggy seated to his right and Pogo on his left. Manson asked what song they wanted to start with. Depending on their proficiency and energy, they might be run through several, including "Sweet Dreams." If they showed promise, Manson inquired after any other musical skills they might possess.

Right before it was Linton's turn to go in, Trent Reznor walked into the waiting area and wished him "Good luck," which the guitarist took as his cue to enter. He strolled into the dimly lit chamber and launched into "Get Your Gunn." "After I played it, I stopped and didn't roll through the rest of the songs. There was a spotlight in my face. It was the only light in the room." The unholy trinity perched on the sofa before him, but Linton couldn't really distinguish their features. "I stopped and walked around the light and talked to them. I think it was probably from that point on that I felt that it was basically done."

But Linton wasn't the only player to pass the first stages of rank and muster. According to candidate Clint Yeager (who got a call from Ciulla saying auditions had been videotaped and would be reviewed in the final selection process), both Twiggy and Manson himself would intimate to him later in the day that he was in the lead. Twiggy ran into him, out drinking with several other potentials, at a bar in the Quarter that night, circa 2 A.M. and confirmed what Ciulla had told him earlier: Manson was interested in speaking with him further.

The next morning, Yeager claims he received a call from Manson at his motel, informing him that while they'd liked his performance, he seemed better suited to rhythm guitar than lead. When Daisy's name came up, Manson went off on a brief tirade, then got back to the subject at hand. "He told me he wanted to have two guitar players—one to play lead and another guy to play rhythm guitar and maybe keyboards and percussion," Yeager said in *Guitar World*. The complexity of the new material dictated that the band needed to either recruit two guitar players, or run a tape during the show; the latter idea held less appeal for Manson. If they opted to go with two guitarists, they'd offer Yeager the rhythm slot. If they only chose one, he was up against two other candidates.

Linton had been out boozing and carousing on Bourbon Street, too, with several other players who'd tried out. He didn't return to his hotel room until after sunrise. "Then I got a call at around 11 o'clock from somebody that sounded as tired, if not more tired, as I was and it was Manson," he told *Guitar World*. They spoke for what seemed like hours, about their favorite musicians, including David Bowie, and Iggy Pop and the Stooges. When they finally hung up, Linton hopped in a cab and met the singer for lunch to chat more.

In early August, the band announced (to the consternation of Yeager) the selection of Timothy Linton as their sole new guitarist. Although Twiggy has joked that part of the audition process was forcing him to play a game of Dungeons & Dragons with the band, Daisy's replacement actually had to undergo a more strenuous test of his fantasy role-playing skills to gain entry. He had to bunk with Manson. "I had him come stay with me in my apartment," Manson told *CMJ New Music Monthly*, "and it was more about we were looking for someone with the right personality because you can find anyone to play guitar. That's only half of it. It's about being part of what we are. I feel that we're whole now. We have what we've always been missing. It was just that little something that was holding us back all these years and now I feel we're strong and I feel we can do what we want to do. And his guitar playing, obviously, was more than adequate. He's a great guitar player." Not too surprisingly, Linton's roots included a stint as a guitar manufacturer; in *Guitar World*, Twiggy claimed Linton had even built an instrument for Iron Maiden's Dave Murray.

"I really liked him before he put his guitar on because of the way he carried himself," Manson added in *Seconds*. And Linton immediately felt like he fit in, image and all. Although some fans and critics were quick to brand the delicate-featured lad a goth, like all true goths he rejected the tag: "The whole goth thing, I think it's pretty cool," he admitted in *Guitar World*. Like Daisy before him, he had a taste for bands like the Cure, Bauhaus, and Siouxsie and the Banshees. "The goth take is kind of weird," he concluded. If folks were leveling the tag at him as a compliment, he wasn't going to get upset.

Linton's new name would be Zim Zum. Although some dedicated fans managed to turn up a fashion model and at least one serial killer who fit into the preexisting pattern, Manson had elected to reject the old system of nomenclature, as yet another significant step in the band's evolution. Paula O'Keefe deduced that this refers to the Kabbalistic term *tzimtzum* or *tsimtsum,* the empty space God made (withdrew his presence from) in the universe, to make room for the creation.

"We felt almost since Marilyn Manson has transformed into Antichrist Superstar," Manson summed up in *Guitar World*, "he became a member of that entity and Zim Zum, unlike the names of the other members of Marilyn Manson, is a Hebrew term that refers to an Angel that was doing God's dirty work at the beginning of time. We felt that since he joined the band to complete this tour and continue on with us that he was doing the dirty work as well."

.   .   .

SPEAKING OF DIRTY WORK, Veronica Kirchoff was at the end of her rope with the fan club, even with her work slowdown in full effect. During the recording of *Antichrist Superstar*, around the same time Daisy exited the ranks, Manson rang her up and announced that management felt she couldn't handle the task alone. They were going to move the operation in-house, to the Cleveland-based Nothing offices. After all of the promises that she'd be rewarded if she just weathered the storm, Kirchoff was stunned. "I'm thinking I'm gonna grow with them, and in one fell swoop, it's all gone.

"Manson said, 'I'm gonna see if you can keep doing the newsletter, because I like the way you write. You're the only person I want to write the newsletter.' " Kirchoff set to closing up shop, taking stock of inventory and back orders, assembling boxes of old letters. She was kept on the payroll through the end of June. "It took that long to get everything finalized." But since the Tacoma mailbox she'd hired was listed as the official fan club address throughout the print media (and cyberspace), the letters kept coming. And she rudely discovered that the USPS doesn't like to forward mail delivered to rented boxes from private vendors. "So I got screwed by that for a while," she sighs, "still doing this work for them."

But Manson seemed to want to make good on his promise to leave the newsletter in her charge. "I talked to Tony [Ciulla] about it while we were tying up the loose ends, and he said, 'Yeah, I'll give you a call when we're ready to do the next newsletter.' " They'd been sending out the original one since the previous autumn. "And I didn't hear anything from anybody for a long time," save for the occasional inquiry regarding the notes and materials she'd turned over. "But no friendly contact with Manson anymore.

"Next time I heard anything was September," she recalls. "Tony called and said, 'We're ready to get going on another newsletter, and Manson says he wants to talk to you directly about what he wants to be in it.'

" 'Well, that'll be nice, since I haven't talked to him since May or June,' " she thought. "After he didn't have a reason that he was obligated to talk to me, he didn't talk to me anymore." She honestly didn't understand why the singer had grown so distant, when in the past they'd spoken frequently. "There were times he'd call me from the road, when they were touring, like, 'I can't take this anymore.' And basically cry on my shoulder. He would call me of his own free will, and all of a sudden he didn't anymore.

"Once I got to know him better, on a personal level, he wouldn't try to hide [his dorky side] anymore," she says. "And I started liking him more, because I got to know him better as a person. That's what made it really difficult when he dropped me."

But Manson never did call again. Kirchoff left Ciulla a phone message, but "never heard anything back from anyone." A couple months later, a new Manson fan club newsletter was delivered to Veronica's sister, who she'd placed on the mailing list out of curiosity. She was not pleased. "It was the ugliest thing . . . somebody had basically taken what I had written, rehashed it, filled in the blanks with some new information, and put in on a page. And on the other side, they put a list of merchandise, folded it up, and mailed it." But despite her disappointment, she'd already stopped attempting to maintain contact with the band, and had ceased forwarding old mail when the petty cash for postage ran out.

"The last time Manson played [Seattle], I didn't even go," she adds. "I contemplated going, but if I saw Manson right now, I'd strangle him. I'm so mad at him." She does admit she occasionally wishes she could sit down with the singer and find out what really transpired. And she still gets a kick out of following his activities in the media, albeit in a much more limited fashion. "There's so much stuff that he's doing now, as far as being a rock star, in the public eye." Veronica finds it especially amusing that Marilyn Manson is now firmly entrenched in the pantheon of alternative rock. "A few years ago, he was totally against stuff like that. But in a way, he's getting what he wanted. He's infiltrating everything. Everybody knows the name Marilyn Manson now, and that was his goal."

TWELVE

THE BAND SPENT THE last months of the summer holed up in a rehearsal space, while Zim Zum learned the new material. The new guitarist made his public debut on September 5, at New York's Irving Plaza, for the Night of Nothing Records portion of the CMJ Music Marathon. After keeping the audience waiting close to an hour after Meat Beat Manifesto's opening set, Marilyn Manson's show lasted a mere five songs, concluding abruptly when the singer brained Ginger with a microphone stand. The drummer crawled away from his kit bleeding profusely, and was quickly whisked off to a nearby medical facility, where he received stitches and then spent the night. At the evening's conclusion, after a Nine Inch Nails performance that saw Trent reunited with former NiN guitarist Richard Patrick (now of Filter), Manson were conspicuously absent from Reznor's thanks extended to the evening's performers.

Was Manson's assault on Ginger deliberate? One witness suspects it may have been. Techno pioneer Moby was watching the show from the wings that night, and says he saw the whole event as it transpired. "They were playing, and it sounded really good," he revealed during an *Alternative Press* round table with Glenn Danzig. "And then the singer, Marilyn, got upset with the drummer. And this really, really bothers me. . . . While the drummer was playing, and not looking, he took a mike stand—which is a heavy piece of metal—and threw it . . . so that the base hit the drummer in his head. I have no problem with self-inflicted violence on stage. Occasionally things go wrong, people jump in the crowd, someone might get hurt. That's okay." Could he have been mistaken? "I was quite close, and watched it. The ambulance had to come and take him away."

Despite his well-known questioning nature, that event turned Moby off Marilyn Manson for good. "I have no patience with bullies," he adds. "My ex-girlfriend grew up with him in Florida, and said that all the kids used to make fun of him because he used to drive this red Fiero, and was really anal about keeping it [spotless]. . . . This was before he became a punk rocker." Someone hurting someone else like this doesn't wash with Moby. "Do whatever you want to yourself. Cut yourself with razor blades, roll on broken glass, cut off your dick on stage, anything—fine. But don't hurt other people. Especially when they can't defend themselves."

Whether Manson had been influenced by watching Trent abuse NiN member Chris Vrenna or came to it all on his own remains subject to debate. But more importantly, why did Fish permit Manson to place him in physical peril on a regular basis? "What else am I going to do?" he retorted in the pages of *Drum*, noting that he'd been unemployed when the band picked him to replace Sara Lee Lucas. Critics thought it might be easy for Fish to depart, but he didn't see it that way. "Everyone's like, 'Just do another project.' But there are a gazillion projects out there that aren't selling out. Manson sells out every single night wherever we go." He was willing to sustain some bruises in exchange for the big money.

ANTICHRIST SUPERSTAR WAS RELEASED on October 8, 1996, and entered the *Billboard* album sales charts at No. 3, just behind Kenny G and Celine Dion. There could be no argument now that the band was firmly established in the mainstream. This time the reviews were much more positive. *Rolling Stone* awarded the album with four stars and a perceptive review by Lorraine Ali. Not that it was greeted roundly with unanimous cheers. While Jim Farber graded the album B in *Entertainment Weekly*, he concluded, "Nihilism this goofy makes one long to be 15 again and naïve enough to swallow such 'satanic' hokum whole."

While some fans mourned the absence of the morbid carnival humor of the first two records, the majority of those who had been waiting dove into the album's thick symbolism. "It is such total deconstruction of anything we understood as 'Marilyn Manson' as to accomplish genuine ego death, magickal [*sic*] dissolution, a state of nonbeing that is stunning and chilling to witness," wrote Paula O'Keefe in her essay "Worms with Angel Wings." There were few recognizable samples, no comic interludes. "I'm not so much into toys and things as I used to be in the past couple of years," Manson observed in *CMJ New Music Monthly* when quizzed on his maturation. The music reflected this disillusion. The man behind *Antichrist Superstar* was a much darker, more serious Manson than anyone had anticipated. "You thought you had Marilyn Manson all wrapped up, it says. Dr. Seuss and KISS and *H. R. Pufnstuf*, sugar addiction and mass murder and child abuse, gender imbalance and guys in drag, with a little trendy Satanism and some bondage outfits for spice. You were wrong."

In the loosest sense of the notion, *Antichrist Superstar* followed the format of a concept album, a semiautobiographical trek through the evolution of the helpless Wormboy (Brian Warner) into the rock star of his dreams (Marilyn Manson). Ultimately, he becomes the larger-than-life title figure (Antichrist Superstar), the embodiment of all the ideals that Marilyn Manson both already did, and would soon come to, represent. But Manson made sure that interviewers understood that the record wasn't intended solely to connect with audiences while the CD player was on. This was meant to serve as "a musical ritual that would bring about the Apocalypse." Which, he was quick to point out in *huH*, didn't necessarily mean Armageddon. "For me, the idea of Antichrist is an unspoken knowledge that every person has, and it's just the denial of God and the acceptance of yourself as a powerful entity that can make their own decisions."

Manson's Antichrist wasn't a small child sent from hell with the numbers 666 hidden on his scalp, and his Apocalypse wasn't the demise of mankind in a hail of fire and brimstone. Rather, he hoped that the record's impact would cleanse his fans, old and new, of all the garbage and debris clogging their spirits and keeping them mired in outmoded social and spiritual conceits. By obliterating the hold of a Christian God over people, he hoped to trigger their own transformation, just as he claimed he had. "I don't care if something's good or bad or if it's Christian or anti-Christian—I want something that's strong, something that believes in itself."

"I watched something the other day on VH-1, it was like the early days of MTV and people were talking about music and its effect on society, and I watched artist after artist say, 'I don't think music can change anything, it's entertainment,' " he told writer Paul Semel. "But I completely disagree. I think, you write a song, and people are singing it, and the things that people hum along to have some resonance." *Antichrist Superstar* aimed for lofty goals, and appeared poised to achieve them.

He also knew his detractors were still numerous. "The people who are afraid of what it's saying will love to dismiss it as a concept record, a fictional story, because that'll make them feel comfortable about it," Manson noted in *CMJ New Music Monthly*. But that was all part of his grand scheme, and he assumed that dedicated Christians, especially the more conservative elements, would play into his hands. "These people are hysterical, you've got the religious angle, and they're gonna say, 'How can you say these things?' "

"What do you have to be afraid of?" he chuckled. "It's just a record . . . or is it?"

The adolescent Marilyn Manson of the past was gone, relegated to the annals of rock history now. "We've grown a lot, and this to me is the definitive Marilyn Manson album, everything that we've been working up to. Everything up to this point was carefully placed stepping-stones. This record to me is much older, it's something that I've wanted to do from the beginning. It was just a matter of the right time, and the right time is now." Understanding Marilyn Manson now was going to be a much more complicated affair, embracing philosophies and concepts that transcended the pop culture dementia that fueled their earlier triumphs. "It might not be as defined as it was before," he said of their new raison d'être.

Among the reference points that Manson hinted would help fans enjoy a deeper understanding of the album were the works of German philosopher Friedrich Nietzsche, whom the singer had been paying homage to since before *POAAF*. But while his previous lyrics had flirted with concepts of Social Darwinism and the spiritual evolution of man, *Antichrist Superstar* seemed to embody many of Nietzsche's concepts; the thinker's *On the Genealogy of Morals* had even spoken of an Antichrist who would triumph over God and nothingness. "This man of the future, who will redeem us not only from the hitherto reigning ideal but also from that which was bound to grow out of it, the great nausea, the will to nothingness, nihilism . . ." Some fans used the philosopher's works as a divining rod to delve into the complex nuances of *Antichrist Superstar*. Manson devotees Jim Kenefick and Donna L. Cross even went so far as to work their interpretations up into "a dual analysis" of the album, entitled *All-American Antichrist*, exploring Nietzschean themes therein. Almost immediately, they noted that in *Thus Spoke Zarathustra*, the philosopher used the symbol of a worm to depict man's evolution from the current state of weakness to the idealized man of the future, the *übermensch*.

The album was neatly divided into three sections, beginning with "Part One: The Heirophant." The arcane word referred to a high priest or seer with visionary powers, with the ability to predict the future. And appropriately enough, the searing opening track, "Irresponsible Hate Anthem," bore the footnote "recorded live on February 14, 1997," a good four months after the record's release date. "It's our Valentine to the world," he joked.

"You actually shouldn't even be able to hear 'Irresponsible Hate Anthem,' so if you can hear it, that means you're definitely in tune with what we're doing," Manson told *Guitar School* in the autumn of 1996, claiming it hadn't been recorded yet. The song's date immediately established the idea of simultaneity that the singer had brought up in his comments to *CMJ New Music Monthly*.

With lyrics like "I hate the hater / I'd rape the raper / I am the animal who will not be himself," the track instantly galvanized the listener. "Just as much as I love things, I hate them," Manson explained, adding that he'd chosen the title because that's exactly what he anticipated detractors labeling it. "The people who would call us hateful are missing the point. And there will be a lot of people who will say they hate us because they'll say we're hateful. They are not seeing their own hypocrisy. These people will be revealed and they'll be fed to the lions." In one blistering assault, he quickly summed up the inherent contradictions riddling the prevailing notions of morality in America.

From there the record shifted into the percussive "The Beautiful People," which was chosen as the first single. "It's all about the fascism of beauty," Manson quipped to *OUT*, "because I'm about as far as you could get from Brad Pitt." But thousands of teenage girls (and boys, for that matter) didn't care, which Manson found curious. "I consider myself the opposite of the archetypal sex symbol," he confessed to *CMJ New Music Monthly*, noting that he wasn't likely to be mistaken for Antonio Banderas any time soon. "But maybe that's the taboo element of my image, which is almost deathlike, is something that attracts them. People always gravitate towards death, because of their fear of it. It exhilarates them." He noted that few sexual taboos remained, even in the era of AIDS. "The only thing that can excite them now is the fear of it being dangerous.

"That song is a statement on the fascism of beauty, with commercialism and television, everything's completely dictated to you, and if you don't fit into the status quo, you're made to feel not as good as everyone else," he continued. "The type of totalitarianism that *Antichrist Superstar* suggests is a group of non-joiners, a crowd of individuals that are all banding together to change what the mainstream is. It actually can't even be described with an '-ism,' because I think it's above and beyond everything that's been attempted in the past. It's like a pep rally for the apocalypse."

"It's not your fault that you're always wrong / The weak ones are there to justify the strong," Manson sang, summarizing the Nietzschean notion of "will to power." And later Manson would compare the lyric "If you live with apes, man, it's hard to be clean" to his struggle with righteous censors. "As much as man looks down upon apes as being a lesser-developed version of himself," he told the online magazine *Allstar,* "that's how I look down upon Christians in America—a sort of lesser form of intelligence."

If "The Beautiful People" hinted at young Brian Warner's earliest initiation to the injustices of the world (a notion the stunning video by Floria Sigismondi, with frightening images of teetering giants, seemed to underscore), then the subsequent "Dried Up, Tied and Dead to the World" seemed to point at the trials of his early family life. With images of fruit and seeds, and lyrics like "Cake on some more makeup / Cover up those lines," Manson appeared to be addressing the institution of motherhood, and parenting in general.

And what was the nature of Manson's relationship with his biological family now? In *Rolling Stone,* Hugh Warner said he called his son Manson ("It's called respect of the artist") these days, while Barbara still elected to address him as Brian. But the singer also insisted to *Guitar School* that she was understanding of her son's actions. "She just feels responsible, so she has no other choice but to just accept it." When pressed on the issue, he hesitated, then gave a little more insight into Barbara's character. "She has mice and she talks to them, and she wakes up in the middle of the night and she has visions of people standing at the foot of her bed—demons and stuff like that."

Hugh Warner made a point of trumpeting his son's achievements frequently in the press. "He's very dedicated, he does 100 percent. And I'm very proud of him—he's the 'God of Fuck,' " he proclaimed in *Alternative Press.* While other parents clamored to decry Manson's music and philosophy, Hugh kept swinging. "He wants parents to raise their children right, and that's probably what's wrong with our society today," the senior Warner noted in *Rolling Stone.* "They don't always give children the freedom or respect they deserve."

The first part of the *Antichrist Superstar* trilogy concluded with "Tourniquet," one of the only songs on which Daisy played lead guitar. Like much of the album's content, the image of the tourniquet carried multiple meanings. On the one hand, a tourniquet can cut off the flow of blood, inducing numbness, and eventually causing permanent damage. But it can also stop the course of something harmful, like poison reaching the heart. Even as the song addressed the pain of being cut off from the love of others, it also reveled in the strength of the individual.

In "Worms with Angel Wings," Paula O'Keefe noted that the triumph of Marilyn Manson had probably minimized any chance he might have for a "normal" romantic involvement in the future. "I've always had these dreams about making a girl out of all these pieces of prosthetic limbs, and then taking my own hair and teeth that I saved from when I was a kid and very ritualistically creating this companion," he told *Rolling Stone*. Those dreams seem linked to his youthful habit of cutting out just the sex organs in pornographic photos, and the violent nightmares of doing it for real that he mentioned later. Interestingly enough, Manson had actually begun collecting prosthetic limbs by this time, too.

O'Keefe also notes that the singer's frequent enticements for the audience to spit on him in concert neatly embodied the sort of love/hate duality at play in the lyric. "When you grow up in America, things like Christianity water down your feelings and dilute a lot of things," Manson had told *RIP* the year before. "When you're taught to love everybody, to love your enemy, what value does that place on love?"

THE SECOND PORTION OF the cycle, "Part Two: Inauguration of the Worm," paralleled the transformation of the hero into the person of his dreams. The segue was provided by the song "Little Horn," which sonically deviated from the quieter nature of the tracks of Part One (save "Irresponsible Hate Anthem," which technically—because of the future dating—stood outside any linear chronology). Manson told *Rolling Stone* the song had been inspired by a recurring dream in which the world was destroyed, and he was the sole survivor. "It was like an ultimate retribution for all of the things that have happened to me growing up." One such dream was set in the future, possibly even in Fort Lauderdale, he surmised. "Entertainment had gone to such an extreme that they had taken people and made them into zombies almost just for entertainment's sake. And I had this strange vision of these women who were completely brain dead—they were just dancing in cages, and their jaws were wired shut so that they wouldn't bite off the dicks of all these guys that were around them masturbating. It was a complete Sodom and Gomorrah." Amidst it all, Manson saw himself, a vague participant or even ringleader in the debauchery. "That was probably the first of what will be Antichrist Superstar rearing its head."

Paula O'Keefe interpreted the song as the star seeing a vision of what lay before him. The imagery was borrowed from the dreams of the biblical prophet Daniel, "who saw a mythic beast rising from the sea having a little horn with eyes like the eyes of man and a mouth speaking great things." The beast with the little horn would bring down the hosts of heaven, just as Manson sought to topple Christianity with *Antichrist Superstar*.

Although Manson claimed in *Guitar School* that the next track, "Cryptorchid," was about his mother, the lyrics don't suggest an immediate connection. The title refers to the condition of having one or both testicles not descended outside the body, as happens in a normal puberty. In this track, the transformation from the worm, Brian Warner, into the rock star, Marilyn Manson, seemed to be complete. Several critics have also noted that this is the song which introduced the lyrical idée fixe "Prick your finger it is done / The moon has now eclipsed the sun / The angel has spread his wings / The time has come for bitter things." Donna L. Cross suggests these lines represent an incantation signaling the exact moment of metamorphosis; they occur again before the album's conclusion.

"Deformography" took the form of a dialogue between different facets of Manson's personality, the wormboy struggling to accept the mantle of the rock star. Meanwhile "I fell into you and I'm on my back / An insect decaying in your little trap" hinted that this evolution was painful and distressing. "I make myself just to poison you / If I can't have you then no one will," he sings, clarifying that his rage is definitely focused inward, extending the Nietzschean concepts further. "The *übermensch* is ultimately creative, destroying only the parts of himself (and by extension, the pieces of society) he needs in order to continue growing," notes scholar Colin McComb. "It's not a destructive urge, a desire to tear all things down."

"Wormboy" was another one of the songs Berkowitz had contributed to, and sonically it recalls *POAAF* more than any other track (which displeased some fans). By referencing the older sound, Manson creates context, and can scrutinize the man he used to be. The singer told *Guitar World* the themes of metamorphosis throughout the album, and in this song in particular, had been spawned by his interest in Social Darwinism. "There's been the theory of man as a worm that then transforms into an ape, and finally into a man." The image of "the undying worm" also appeared in Milton's epic poem *Paradise Lost.* "[The Book of] Revelations also speaks a lot about the worm, and man's pupa stage. But I look on it as being both a beginning and an end," he clarified.

"Mister Superstar" had been written before the band had broken through with "Sweet Dreams," yet the song seemed an ideal commentary on their success. "Hey Mr. Fallen Star, don't you know I worship you?" he howled. The former Brian Warner had finally realized his dreams, only to discover they couldn't wholly satisfy him. The adoration of millions only seemed to make the bile rise in his throat. "I know that I can turn you on / I wish I could just turn you off / I never wanted this / I never never never wanted any of this . . ." "I was almost speaking to myself, as much as I was speaking to the people around me," he confessed in *CMJ New Music Monthly.* And as Paula O'Keefe noted, the internal debate continued to rage on; if you listen closely with headphones, you can hear a chilling interplay between the two stereo channels, as one voice drones, "I wish I was dead," while a whisper answers back, "Kill yourself on TV."

"Angel with the Scabbed Wings" featured Danny Lohner from Nine Inch Nails on lead guitar. Lyrically Manson seemed to be lashing out at his fans for blind adoration: " 'He is the maker' / (He is the taker) / 'He is the savior' / (He is the raper)." Colin McComb notes that to concern himself with the opinions of others would represent a departure from the Nietzschean underpinnings. "The *übermensch* feels no responsibility for the herd that follows him," he writes. "He doesn't care what they think." Whether or not the trappings of fame troubled him, Manson was nothing if not gracious to his fans.

"Kinderfeld" (a German term that translates as "field of children") had originally been slated for inclusion on *Smells Like Children,* but fit in thematically with *Antichrist Superstar* far better. It was filled with disturbing images of an old man named Jack, with "cracked and dirty" hands and fingernails like "beetle wings," who plays with a toy train set. The inspiration was obvious to anyone familiar with Manson's childhood. "It talks about the point where the axis shifted, and I feel like I went from being a worm into something else," he confirmed in *CMJ New Music Monthly*. "And that's the moment in the song where I'm watching my grandfather, who kind of became a metaphor for hypocrisy, the hidden filth in what was assumed to be innocent." Manson still identified with his childhood, but not in a way that collecting lunch boxes or action figures could soothe.

"And at the end of the song, I almost see things through his eyes, so I almost become him. And that's when things start going the other direction. That's an important moment on the record." The transformation into the Antichrist Superstar was almost complete. "Then I got my wings and I never even knew it / When I was a worm I thought I couldn't get through it," he sang. (An odd side note: Donna L. Cross notes that the phrase "I'll have to kneel on broomsticks" refers to an old Christian act of atonement and repentance.)

THE FINAL THIRD OF the record, "Disintegrator Rising," delved even further into philosophical themes. Marilyn Manson, the Antichrist Superstar, was being swept up by the winds of a success that could only continue to increase. But the dissection of strengths and weaknesses wasn't entirely intended for public consumption: that was merely a side effect of Manson's constant self-analysis. "The *übermensch* doesn't care about making others follow his lead, except insofar as doing so contributes to his own aims," notes McComb. Committing an act simply for the sake of doing it was neither a part of Nietzsche's directive, nor Manson's.

According to *Guitar World*, the title track featured more than twenty-seven rhythm tracks, including five of lead guitars. Once again, the incantation "prick your finger / it is done" appeared, heralding the conclusion of yet another transformation, from the rock star Marilyn Manson into something much greater, the Antichrist

Superstar. He leveled the finger of blame at the world that had spawned him. "You built me up with your wishing hell / I didn't have to sell you . . . whose mistake am I anyway?" The lyrics raised the question, Would Marilyn Manson exist in Utopia? "In the world that I envision, Marilyn Manson isn't necessary," he commented to Paul Semel. "However, that's not the world we live in."

But despite his grim outlook throughout the album, he also insisted that the mantle he'd accepted didn't really cause him the agony his lyrics suggested. "I do enjoy doing what I do, and I do enjoy who I am, so in no way am I ever complaining about having to accept this role," he continued in *huH*. "In the end, it is music, and it is for people's entertainment, and it is to be enjoyed, and it is to inspire people to do their own thing and be creative in their own way." Nothing pleased him more than the notion that his art might inspire others to delve into their own creativity.

"1996" had purportedly been composed the same night of the infamous human bone-smoking prank. "Anti fascist / anti mod / I am the anti-music god," Manson proclaimed, staking out the alpha and omega nature of the Antichrist Superstar, Nietzsche's hyper-evolved *übermensch*. But the quiet "Minute of Decay" that followed stressed how much self-loathing success had spawned in Manson. "I'm on my way down, I'd like to take you with me. . . ." The singer had given so much of himself, he felt he might not have anything of merit left to offer.

The penultimate track, "The Reflecting God," acknowledged that Manson recognized that the full scope of the complex messages encoded in *Antichrist Superstar* might very well elude many listeners. "I say it is and then it's true / There is a dream inside a dream / I'm wide awake the more I sleep / You'll understand when I'm dead." The idea of being understood posthumously was yet another nod to Nietzsche, in this case the introduction to the text *The Antichrist*. And while the song extended "no salvation, no forgiveness," that salvo was only directed at those who had allowed themselves to remain weak. "One shouldn't pity those who allow themselves the indulgence of weakness," says McComb, adding that this sentiment "doesn't mean pissing on everyone less than you."

"That song has a weird emotion," Manson noted in *CMJ New Music Monthly* of the final cut, "Man That You Fear." "It's not depressing . . . I don't know what it is," he sighed. "It's an acceptance, really." On one level, the lyrics spun out the remorse of a dying man who feels he's somehow failed. Yet they could also be read as a condemnation of society, and the Christian church in particular. "You've poisoned all your children to camouflage your scars."

After a moment of silence following the fade of "Man That You Fear," the hidden track number 99 kicked in. A distorted voice repeats the looped line "When all of your wishes are granted, many of your dreams will be destroyed." Just as Nietzsche had believed in the idea of an eternal recurrence, Manson realized that the messages of the Antichrist weren't new by any stretch of the imagination. "When Nietzsche said eternal recurrence, he meant that all things come back," writes McComb. "Just the same. The point being, live your life as you find pleasure in living it—imagine living it over and over and over again *ad nauseam*."

"ANTICHRIST SUPERSTAR IS TO me the empowered . . . sort of king figure, the final evolution of Marilyn Manson that we may not even have gotten to yet," the singer concluded in *CMJ New Music Monthly*. "I went through a transformation in the record, but I also feel like that transformation happens on a daily basis. And on a lifetime scale, it still hasn't completed itself yet." There were prophetic moments that spoke of events in Manson's life that hadn't occurred yet. He wasn't afraid to speak on such an ambitious scale, even if a vast majority of people didn't understand. "I've always done this, and I've always gotten flack for this from everyone that I work with: the label, even to working with Trent. I've always seen things as being where they are now, and I see things farther ahead. Sometimes I get ahead of myself, and I say, 'Well, I need to do this, because that's how I'm gonna put myself here.' And maybe other people haven't had the same faith or belief in what I do, but I've always been quite convinced of where this would go." And *Antichrist Superstar* was going to deliver him to that destination.

Thirteen

THE HOTLY ANTICIPATED "DEAD to the World" tour kicked off on October 3, 1996 (five days before the actual release of *ACS*) at the State Theater in Kalamazoo, Michigan. The relatively lackluster downtown Manhattan quartet N.Y. Loose opened on the first leg of the long journey. By far their most ambitious outing to date, the tour was scheduled to last eighteen months, and take the band around the globe, to South America, Europe, Japan, and Australia. Utilizing countless audio, visual, and lighting cues, plus prerecorded material that all had to be in sync, it was hardly the easiest show to get up and running. Technical snafus and frazzled nerves meant that some of the early concerts had to be cut short. But once the bugs had been worked out, it surpassed anything the band (and most of their peers) had ever delivered.

The stage production proved exceptionally impressive, featuring an enormous backdrop designed as a ruined church, including a pipe organ for Pogo. In the background, framed by impaled angels ("Try finding that at Home Depot," quipped *CMJ New Music Monthly*), a female angel wrestled with Satan. Manson delivered portions of the show from a giant pulpit, and the ambitious costume changes were carefully choreographed, right down to the steel combat helmets. A snow machine added to the eerie ambience of the finale. "It's a weird choice for us to end the show with 'Man That You Fear,'" Manson observed in *New Music Monthly*, "but that's the way that I ended the record, and that's the final thing that I have to say." Carefully structured to reflect the contours of *ACS*, without neglecting older fan favorites, the show captured the greater emotional breadth of the new album.

"An album you spend forever on, but it's really just a blueprint for a performance," he continued. More so than in the studio, he felt completely at home on the stage. And recognizing how long the show would be on the road, he wanted to ensure it would remain just as exciting for the band as for the fans. "I like to step on stage, and feel as overwhelmed as somebody in the audience would. And I do.

"In the second half of the show, I feel just as empowered as those people do, a part of it." Indeed, midway into the set, the audience became charged with a palpable energy, as banners unfurled and Manson climbed into the podium, and the band ripped into "The Beautiful People." "That moment is actually a statement on the relationship between performers and their audiences, totalitarianism, fascism, things like that," prompting at least one critic to refer to the spectacle as "T. Rex at Nuremberg." "Obviously the church transforms into the fascist dictatorship there, so it's also a statement on religion as well," Manson noted of the sudden shift in the show's direction. "And it's one that's meant to confuse, and make people leave the show with questions."

He did make sure, however, to clarify that this was in no way, shape, or form a pro-Nazi statement. "Because that's actually the polar opposite of individuality." Even if the new *ACS* lightning bolt emblem suggested the Nazi SS symbol (which already formed part of the famous KISS logo). "It is simply the international symbol for 'danger of electric shock,' universally used on electrical appliances and equipment," Paula O'Keefe noted later.

Much to Manson's consternation, some fans had misinterpreted at least one essential message encoded in *Antichrist Superstar*. Just because Marilyn Manson—as they had previously been incarnated—had come to an end, the band was not splitting up, nor was Manson going to destroy himself. Yet rumors had been circulating now for up to a year that the singer was going to commit suicide onstage at the band's Halloween show at Convention Hall in Asbury Park, New Jersey. Younger aficionados probably weren't aware that identical tall tales had long dogged other shock rock superstars, from Iggy Pop to G. G. Allin. But even though Mr. Manson stated, repeatedly, he wasn't going to commit such an act, the whispering continued. In the end, the show that evening was held up by a bomb threat. "I guess someone thought they would take care of the situation for me," he told Neil Strauss in *Rolling Stone*.

The tour wound through the Midwest, then down the East Coast, heading down to the South. After a show at the Sunrise Musical Theatre in Miami on November 16, the band took a week off before heading to South America. During this time, the band hooked up with their friends in Smashing Pumpkins (purportedly convincing Billy Corgan to snort sea monkeys one delirious evening). But they also ran into old acquaintances of a different stripe. Scott Mitchell, the former Daisy Berkowitz, had gone down to Miami with a friend to enjoy some time off. They had opted to hang out at a club called Groove Jet. They knew the venue was hosting a Smashing Pumpkins after-party, but thought nothing of it. "You figure, a really big band, after-show party, there's just gonna be a few people there that had just come from the show, and the club's gonna give away shirts," Mitchell chuckles. But when he saw Corgan stride in, he knew the fete might be bigger than he'd realized. Sure enough, his old band mates began to wander in. Still stinging from Manson's comments on *120 Minutes*, the guitarist decided to approach his old partner. "I got around to Mr. Manson, and he loosely apologized, regarding that comment, saying he'd been drinking. I just wanted to see what he'd say. Because I did have a desire to punch him, but I'm a little too cool to let that take advantage of me."

The band departed for South America soon after, playing dates in Santiago, Chile, and Buenos Aires. Manson joked that his potential success below the equator might hinge on "the whole 'Evita' thing" (referring to the balcony scene in "The Beautiful People" video), but appreciated that South American audiences were well known for their vocal support of hard rock acts, especially outrageous, theatrical ones. "America used to be that way, pre-Nirvana," he noted in *New Music Monthly*, "and I think we're coming back to that era. Without being self-aggrandizing, I've seen the little tidal waves that I've caused in the music industry, and how people are becoming more evolved in their imagery, and there are lots of new Marilyn Manson-esque people." But didn't bother him, because he knew that he had come first, and thus stood head and shoulders above his imitators. "There's one real Santa Claus," he quipped, "but there's a lot of fake ones at the mall."

WHILE THE FIRST LEG of the tour had gone reasonably smoothly, "moral outrage" concerning the band from certain public quarters began to escalate in December. Wrapping up a series of fourteen European shows with four UK dates, Manson found themselves being forced to move shows to new venues due to pressure from dissatisfied citizens. Shows at the London Astoria on December 12 and the Glasgow Garage on December 14 eventually went off fine, but a gig scheduled for the day in between, slated at Nottingham Rock City, was called off.

Meanwhile, things at home were also heating up. The former MCA Music Entertainment group (recently renamed Universal Music Group) and their parent company, Seagram Company Limited, found themselves on the receiving end of some harsh criticism from Democratic senator Joseph Lieberman of Connecticut, the National Political Congress of Black Women, and conservative political advocacy group Empower America. When Seagram acquired 50 percent of Interscope Records from Time Warner, who'd buckled to similar pressure from advocacy groups to put their share on the block the year before, they also bought into the brouhaha that comes with a catalog that includes both the Nothing and Death Row Records labels.

At a December 10 press conference held in Washington, D.C., Lieberman, NPCBW chair C. DeLores Tucker (a well known enemy of rap), and Empower America codirector (and former secretary of education) William Bennett blasted Seagram CEO Edgar Bronfman Jr. for his failure to curtail the release of albums they deemed objectionable. Among the artists singled out were Crucial Conflict, Snoop Doggy Dogg, Makaveli (aka Tupac Shakur), and, of course, Marilyn Manson, whom Lieberman decried as "perhaps the sickest artist ever promoted by a mainstream record company." The three made their presentation before an enlargement of the *Antichrist Superstar* back cover art, which depicted Twiggy and Pogo inhaling from face mask hoses attached to Mr. Manson's strap-on dildo. CNN broadcast the press conference, giving Manson some of their widest-reaching publicity to date.

Lieberman (who apparently assumed all Americans are Christian) expressed grave concern that as the nation headed to the malls in the next few weeks, they would be alarmed to see "Silver Bells" rubbing shoulders with songs like "Irresponsible Hate Anthem," as well as countless other tracks "that explicitly and brazenly celebrate murder, rape, torture, and drug use and denigrate our fundamental values." He went on to insist that when MCA had bought into Interscope, they'd pledged to "draw some basic lines of decency and refuse to violate them." But this holy trinity felt that the entertainment conglomerate hadn't lived up to that promise.

"The moguls of the record industry must be made to understand the harm they are inflicting on our children," added C. DeLores Tucker. "They must begin to put principle before profit and stop pimping pornography, drugs, and violence to America's children." But the band's label stood strong behind them. And Manson himself, when quizzed on Tucker's animosity toward the band in an interview for *Guitar School* a few months later, responded with characteristic black humor. "I think she was backstage at one of the shows trying to give blow jobs to one of the crew, but I might be wrong about that."

AS IF ON CUE following that debacle, the New Year brought with it one of the oddest announcements in the Manson annals yet, when rapper Snoop Doggy Dogg revealed to *SPIN* that he was planning to remix "The Beautiful People." He and Manson had met at the MTV Video Awards the previous fall, and gotten on like a house on fire. Although he admitted he wasn't familiar with the rest of Manson's oeuvre, Snoop referred to the clip for "The Beautiful People" as "some dope shit." He even planned to do his own video for the song (although he stressed that he wouldn't do drag or wear makeup in it), and was considering inviting Manson to guest on his upcoming album. (Sadly, the collaboration never seemed to take off. "That's something I would still love to do," Manson commented nine months later. "Since his tour was as hectic as mine, it hasn't happened yet. But it's not to say it won't.")

And as his notoriety and popularity surged, Manson was garnering increasing kudos in critical circles. The January 23, 1997, issue of *Rolling Stone* proclaimed Marilyn Manson their Artist of the Year. The great man was the subject of a thoroughly detailed, highly revealing piece of journalism by *New York Times* critic Neil Strauss, who spent a week with his subject on Manson's home turf in Fort Lauderdale during their break before going to South America. "This is going to be an important piece of press," he noted in one of the earliest of many interviews. Manson was determined to try and clarify all the complex ideas surrounding the album, his persona, and the band's accession.

Naturally, one of the biggest topics addressed was the delineation between the personalities of Marilyn Manson, Antichrist Superstar, and the man formerly known as Brian Warner. "When people sometimes misconceive us as being like KISS or like Alice Cooper, of being a persona, I don't think they understand how deeply Marilyn Manson goes into my existence," he told Strauss.

"My whole take on anything is, I find it completely boring to be one person," he had noted in *New Music Monthly* earlier. Simple-minded people can only see personalities defined in black and white, good and evil. Outsiders wanted to believe that Marilyn Manson was nothing but theater of the highest order, prompted only by a lust for money. "But who's putting the show on?" Manson asked. "I'm very much a part of everything I do, all the time." With the emergence of Antichrist Superstar, there were now "roles within roles," all dovetailing together. "It's so involved, I think it's just a reflection of how people's real personalities are." It was almost as if Manson's physical body was a prism, and the different facets of his personality were revealed as the light of experience passed through him from shifting angles.

"You can't be exactly what you are onstage all the time you're offstage," he also noted in *Guitar World*. "Because then going onstage would no longer be an outlet for you. Your volume knob can't be on 10 at all times."

If you didn't choose to accept that the Warner/Manson/Antichrist setup wasn't all an act, then the signs did begin to resemble the onset of multiple personality disorder (especially when Manson took to speaking of Antichrist Superstar in the third person). An interviewer for *Details* wondered if Manson had ever bothered to seek psychiatric care. "No," came back the answer. "But I've been told by psychologists that I suffer from a condition called the delusion of self. It's when you feel that everything is related and all circumstances have something to do with one another. Some people think of it as a mental disorder, but I just think of it as a higher plane of awareness."

And while Daisy Berkowitz might have quibbled with how sincere Marilyn Manson was, other parties around him suffered no such reservations. "I believe that he believes in what he believes in, he is an Antichrist. Maybe not the biblical one, but then neither was Jesus the 'biblical' King of the Jews that they were looking for," notes a member of the Manson road crew. "I would never, never, never ever call him by his birth name. That was long ago, and it might be his name again some time in the distant future when he is an old man, but he is Marilyn Manson . . . no doubt."

BUT AS THE BAND continued to scale higher and higher in public awareness, the conflicts with concerned Christians and other right-wing advocacy groups only grew exponentially. A January gig at Salt Lake City's Fairpark Coliseum was canceled on the grounds that it promoted values contrary to those held by decent members of the community. A February 5 show in Oklahoma City was protested by a chapter of the American Family Association. And even though Rusty Warren of the *AFA Journal* claims that the "AFA has not, and is not, coordinating any kind of organized effort against the band," protests from affiliates of the parent group continued to proliferate.

In Wheeling, West Virginia, ten days later, the presence of a news crew from CNN's *American Edge* program only seemed to fan the flames between the various factions. Across the street from the Wheeling Civic Center, one congregation held a prayer vigil on the sidewalk, even as a horde of teens in garish makeup mocked them and mugged for the cameras. Meanwhile, a local group associated with the AFA held a free "family celebration," attended by between 250 and 300 folks, as an alternative to the debauchery of the Manson show. "Nothing has ever brought the Christian community together in our valley like opposition to this concert," organizer Kathleen O'Conner, president of a local AFA affiliate in Wheeling, told the *AFA Journal*. (The paper notes she was encouraged to continue these gatherings of "song, prayer, food and fun;" perhaps Wheeling could benefit from a bowling alley or mini-golf franchise.) But while the band's message was offensive to them, the Christians tried to show kindness. "We're not mad at him," O'Conner insisted. "In fact, our hearts go out to him and to any of the children that take his lead."

After a show on February 21, in Fitchburg, Massachusetts, the band took some time off in New York City before heading back out again in early March. The thirty-ninth Grammy Awards took place on February 26, and Manson made a cameo at a party thrown by Interscope, where he fulfilled another one of his fantasies. At the conclusion of his *New Music Monthly* interview back in October, he'd mentioned that he aspired to one day play Nick Cave to Fiona Apple's Kylie Minogue (the sinister singer Cave had scored a hit duet with the international pop tart earlier in the year, stunning music fans). Sure enough, America's favorite sullen teen singer was at the same fete at the Four Seasons bar.

New York poet and publicist Nicole Blackman attended the party that evening with two friends of hers (one of whom was David Lynch's assistant—and Veronica Kirchoff's pal—Jennifer Syme) who were already close to the Manson entourage. The singer was seated at a round booth, entertaining friends, and Fiona Apple was perching on the edge. "I saw the two of them sitting there and could not decide who was skinnier than the other," Blackman admits. "Manson's standing there very regal and royal in his skinniness, while Fiona is all curled up, looking like she was trying to hide. I looked at him and looked at her, and thought, 'I can't decide which one of them needs a sandwich more.' I contemplated going over to the catering table and bringing them something big and heavy and creamy with a lot of mayonnaise and egg in it. And I'd actually seen Twiggy walking out with Courtney Love a few minutes earlier, so obviously [Manson] didn't require baby-sitting."

Not having been introduced, Blackman wasn't about to break the ice with a barbed wisecrack. But a minute later, one of her partners in crime made introductions. "And apparently, when my friend interrupted Marilyn to say 'hello,' he became a little perturbed, because he was trying to get Fiona's attention." During the interruption, celebrated young magician David Blaine approached Apple and impressed her with some sleight of hand. (The two quickly became enamored of each other, and subsequently became a very visible item in the press.) "So that was a sad moment for Marilyn," Blackman concedes.

(While their meeting may not have blossomed into romance, they did remain pals. "He's great," the tortured teen chanteuse later revealed to *Details* magazine. "The funniest sound I've heard in the past year is when Mom yelled, 'Sweetie, Marilyn Manson's on the phone!' ")

Her friend Jennifer introduced Nicole to the singer. "And he stops talking and narrows his eyes and goes, 'Nicole Blackman?' I considered shooting back, 'Yeah, do I owe you money?' " But in fact, he disclosed that he'd been listening to the album *Dead Inside*, her chilling collaboration with Anton Fier under his Golden Palominos umbrella. Blackman had passed along a copy to their mutual friend Sean Beavan, who happened to be handling sound chores on the "Dead to the World" tour, and took to playing it before shows. Manson had been quite taken with the poet's unwavering vision and arresting delivery, even to the point of purchasing multiple copies.

"Apparently he'd bought it for a couple friends for Christmas presents," she recalls. "Which I thought was sort of an odd gift. But then again, I give handcuffs for Christmas presents. I gave my mother an illustrated copy of *The Story of 'O'* one year. We live in exotic times."

"I thought it was very sweet, because he didn't have to say that," she notes the compliment. The Palominos' *Dead Inside* and *Antichrist Superstar* had been released on the same day, and the downtown NYC Tower Records had opted to display them side by side, since their red, white, and (predominantly) black color schemes complemented each other. "They looked kind of nice as little companion pieces," Blackman recalls of seeing them next to each other that first night. "They get along famously. My CD was humping his CD . . . mine was on top, of course," she adds with a laugh.

The two found that their circle of friends intersected at many points, and their paths crossed frequently over the next few months. That summer, after a show, Manson made an odd confession to Blackman. "He told me that he liked to have sex to [*Dead Inside*]. Which sort of perturbed me," she admits. "I think he was befuddled by my reaction. But hearing that somebody likes to have sex to your record is like having somebody house-sit for you and finding out they had a big orgy in your bed and didn't bother to change the sheets."

Manson also made his film debut right around the same time, as David Lynch's *Lost Highway* opened across the country in the last weeks of February. The film, starring Bill Pullman, Patricia Arquette, and Balthazar Getty, was described as a "psychogenic fugue," in which ideas and themes were "introduced in one voice, developed in another." He and Twiggy both appeared as actors in a seedy porno film within the film, watching as Arquette petted another actress, then had her nipples licked.

The movie sound track, overseen by Lynch (who'd videotaped Manson gigs previously) and Trent Reznor (who took pains to dispel rumors that the director had wanted Manson more involved in the sound track), included both "I Put a Spell on You" and a new song, entitled "Apple of Sodom." "There's a song that is very much a part of *Antichrist Superstar,* but it's not on the album," he had mentioned to *Alternative Press* pertaining to the previously unreleased track. With lyrics such as "take this from me/hate me, hate me," "Apple of Sodom" seemed to fit fairly late into the *Antichrist Superstar* cycle. The line "I've got something you could never eat" undoubtedly refers to the real "Apple of Sodom," better known as thorny popolo, a toxic fruit found in Hawaii. Consuming the thorny popolo can result in collapse, paralysis, severe tremors, and even death in a deep coma.

The band also surfaced on another sound track a few weeks later, when *Private Parts,* the humorous biopic of radio shock jock Howard Stern, premiered nationwide on March 7. This time Manson's contribution was "The Suck for Your Solution," a new composition credited to Manson, Twiggy, and Zim Zum (garnering his first writing credit). With angry exclamations of "I suffer for you, I suffer for you/I've suffered for you since the day I was made," the song could be an extension of the *Antichrist Superstar* body of work. But overall the lyrics also tie in nicely with Stern's own story as a controversial media figure who opposed authority to garner a devoted following.

THE BAND RESUMED THEIR travels with a jaunt to Alaska, followed by four dates in Japan, two in Australia, and one in New Zealand. On their way back, they stopped to do a show at the Nimitz Concert Hall in Honolulu, Hawaii, on Saturday, March 22. But things quickly went awry once the band hit the stage, when roughly forty-five minutes into the set Manson suddenly collapsed and had to be rushed to the hospital by ambulance. The specific reason why he'd passed out, however, initially was shrouded in mystery. Mari Matsuoka of Goldenvoice, which promoted the show, said to the press that "he cut himself and there was more blood than expected. We think he hit a vein or something, and was taken to emergency. The EMTs came and then the ambulance came and he was taken to the hospital." But a conflicting report ran in the *Honolulu Advertiser* on Sunday, in which a Manson spokesperson said that the singer (who performed in a corset throughout the Dead tour) had fainted because of hyperventilation and/or exhaustion from their travels.

Considering that Manson had stopped deliberately slicing himself up on stage during shows, the mystery as to how the star might have gotten cut was perplexing. Several months later, the issue was cleared up in an interview with Murray Engleheart for the *Allstar* on-line news service. The whole thing had been a freak mishap. "There was some broken glass on the stage and I'd fallen down on it," he explained. "It went through my hand and hit an artery so it was bleeding really bad, and I would have probably bled to death if I hadn't stopped the show and gone to hospital and had it stitched up." However, it wasn't a suicide attempt (as some rumors speculated), "although Hawaii is the type of place that would make you want to kill yourself if you're like me and dislike sunshine and happiness and people enjoying themselves."

But as the tour commenced its trek across mainstream America, zigzagging between the Midwest and the South before snaking up the East Coast again, resistance from Christian advocacy groups continued to be encountered. Protests and official interference cropped up in cities including La Crosse, Wisconsin, and Biloxi, Mississippi. It seemed increasingly apparent that the protesters were organizing, using a mix of old-fashioned evangelism and contemporary high-tech communication to proliferate defamatory information about the band and ways to hinder their progress. "People were clearly sent, faxed or E-mailed information here," Will Berkheiser, general manager of the Utica Memorial Auditorium, announced in an article on the protests in *Rolling Stone*. (In fact, that May 6 demonstration in Utica, New York, had been spurred on by information sent out by William Bennett's Empower America.)

Erroneous information about Marilyn Manson was constantly coursing through cyberspace. In the past, the band had been dogged by all sorts of bizarre stories: that Manson had cut off his testicles; he'd had ribs removed so he could perform fellatio on himself; that he'd died of a drug overdose in Phoenix; that he'd appeared as a child actor on *Mr. Belvedere* and *The Wonder Years*. Yet by and large, those rumors had been started by fans, whether older Spooks or neophyte Sweet Dreamers. Obviously, very little of the gossip, no matter how outrageous, was spread with malicious intent. Younger fans, with fewer filters, were enthusiastic to learn anything new about their favorite star. "I don't know if gullible is the right word; I think it's more, 'You know what I heard?' noted Manson publicist Jennie Boddy in an *Alternative Press* report on misinformation on popular bands on the Web. "Everyone wants to be the first to tell someone something," she concluded.

Yet the source of the misinformation the protesters were reacting to was much more sinister. In March and April, an unspecified Christian organization had posted on-line a series of "affidavits" (which weren't part of any legal action, but were merely presented as documents verified to be truthful) about the content of Marilyn Manson concerts. Among the allegations listed were claims that Manson had a team of "private Santa Clauses" who sowed the entire audience with free bags of marijuana and cocaine; that chickens, puppies, and kittens had been thrown into the audience, to be slaughtered and offered up in sacrifice to the band; that Manson called for virgin sacrifices; even that frenzied crowds had brutally raped female fans during shows, while Manson egged them on.

Admittedly, to some gentle souls, Manson's real onstage antics—such as using the American flag to wipe his ass, or shredding Bibles—were pretty severe. But the claims listed in the affidavits were out and out falsehoods. Although no organization would claim credit for them, the allegations were purportedly based on sworn testimonies (though nobody came forward to say from whom), and wound up on the Web site of the Gulf Coast branch of the American Family Association.

"Generally I haven't found the Internet useful as a source of reliable information," insists Rusty Benson, associate editor of the American Family Association's monthly *AFA Journal*. "The national organization had nothing to do with the alleged affidavits." In fact, while AFA leader Donald Wildmon and his colleagues had become extremely vocal about their dissatisfaction with Manson, Benson repeated that the "AFA is NOT involved in a 'campaign' against Marilyn Manson. We have simply written several short news stories about the band, pulling information and quotes from a variety of published sources." The purpose of which was to "encourage parents to be aware of what their kids are listening to and consider the potential impact on their lives."

While the grand poobahs of the Manson organization figured out how to handle the impact of the affidavits, the fans went into action for themselves. Paula O'Keefe had dealt with protesters at shows on past tours, and even taken to collecting "their little Jesus flyers." But then someone brought the on-line affidavits to her attention, and she read them in shock. "These were just completely outrageous lies," she recalls. "It would've been funny if they hadn't been presenting it as truth, and especially if they hadn't been posting this stuff with the aim of convincing other people that this is what happens at Manson shows.

"At the end, they said that they were looking for the truth, if anything here was incorrect they wanted to hear about it," she adds. "They were probably just trying to draw us out, but we went for it." A small legion of longtime fans fired off E-mails trying to clarify all the falsehoods. "And some people got messages back, some did not, but about three weeks later, after a good deal of waffling, they posted to their Web site that the accounts had now been confirmed, they could guarantee they were true.

"That completely outraged me. That's when I snapped. They were not only slandering Manson, they were ignoring all these honest people, who had no reason to trust an enemy but had gone in there and told the truth. Here's this bunch of outcast, rat pack kids, atheists and pagans and Satanists and agnostics and gosh knows what, showing every bit as much honesty and decency and integrity as these supposedly upright, white Christian guys weren't! I completely blew up at that point. I declared war. I was not having any more of this. It was bad enough they were treating Manson that way, but they could not treat us that way as well."

Resistance manifested itself in as many different forms as there are types of Manson fans. Some fired off letters to the Christian Family Network, who had "a great anti-Manson website" that detailed the recent concert in Dayton, Ohio ("they can't imagine the pit of hell looking any worse," is the description of the show O'Keefe recalls). Others started up regional chapters of the Portrait of an American

Family Association, serving as clearinghouses for correct information and ideas on how to strike back. O'Keefe began directly confronting protesters when they interfered with her at concerts. "I think it's important for them to realize we're not just a bunch of boneheaded metalheads, that we've done our homework." She, Damian Clement, and some of their colleagues also delved deep into biblical Scripture, and assembled a flyer that looked like the Christian ones, but instead argued a pro-Manson stance with passages from the Good Book and impassioned but tempered essays. Announcing "Understand Us by Understanding Yourself" on the cover, the flyer attempted to dispel rumors, and pointed out to the resistance the very un-Christian elements of their activities.

"The mental image they seem to have is that we're all just kind of misled. That we're ignorant, and being pulled along the path to Satan by this conniving master showman, and that we don't know what we're doing." Enemies of Manson seem to forget that following his music and philosophy is a conscious choice. "Whether you're a Satanist or a pagan or you don't believe in God at all, whether you have no interest in any concept of deity, this is not something you just decided to pick up because Marilyn Manson said so. I'm sure there are kids out there who have done that, but that's for them."

More often than not, O'Keefe is greeted with shock when she hands those who have come to save her soul her own literature on the subject, and engages them in civil conversation. "You can't talk them out of it, because they're set in their ways, but I think just realizing they have some form of intelligent opposition gives them pause. It has at some of the shows I've tried it at." And she's noted that it's rarely young parishioners turning out to fight her. "Usually it's people who look like grade school teachers," the forty-two-year-old laughs. "I don't really expect to get intelligent discourse out of them. The most I ever got was somebody who apologized for attacking us without having really researched what was going on. Which was unusually generous, I thought. The only thing we can hope to do is just point out to them that they're not just dealing with a bunch of brainwashed teenagers here. A lot of us have already decided to what degree we want to be saved, and from what."

The Spooky Kids weren't alone in their fight, either. Regardless of their feelings for the band's music or antics, proponents of free speech of all stripes came out in support of Marilyn Manson. In an article concerning censorship in *Alternative Press* several months later, former Nirvana bassist/Sweet 75 guitarist Krist Novoselic—who founded the Seattle-based Joint Artists and Music Promotions Action Committee to battle such enemies of music—had this to say regarding Manson's various struggles. "Marilyn Manson just provoke a reaction," he told writer Rickey Wright. "They're not lying; they're telling the truth: 'We're gross, we're disgusting, we're vulgar.' People who want to get it, though, should be able to get it. They have a right to make some noise about that."

Now the protests began snowballing into cancellations. A date set for early April in Jackson, Mississippi, was pulled due to poor ticket sales. On April 10, a show scheduled to take place at the Carolina Coliseum in Columbia, South Carolina, was yanked when officials deemed the show "needlessly offensive and dehumanizing." Manson was purportedly paid forty thousand dollars not to perform. In retaliation, the Massachusetts Music Industry Coalition, a nonprofit organization devoted to the protection and promotion of freedom of musical expression, asked fans to E-mail assorted South Carolina politicians at the state and federal level in protest.

Hot on the heels of that announcement, Virginia's state capital, Richmond, also pulled the plug on the quintet's traveling show. A date had been set for May 10 at a city-owned auditorium, but local leaders revealed they felt Marilyn Manson was "just not consistent with our community standards." The local chapter of the American Civil Liberties Union promptly threatened to sue on behalf of Manson fans in the region. But a few days later, on April 21, the Richmond City Council overturned the city manager's decision to ban the concert, after a two-hour, closed-door deliberation on the matter. The concession was that if the ACLU did file suit, the city could not win the battle. The *Richmond Times-Dispatch* also reported that Mayor Larry E. Chavis said that the city extended a financial reward if Manson would bypass Richmond. This time, the band said no.

"Though the popular pressure was to cancel the show, it's against the First Amendment," Kent Willis, the executive director of the ACLU of Virginia, told the press. The ACLU had been ready to file in federal court when the city attorney called and asked them to wait until after the council meeting. According to Willis, the debate had originally begun when a citizen came to a council meeting on April 14 with a copy of Manson's lyrics and said that Manson was "raunchy and misogynist," which seemed sufficient grounds for City Manager Robert C. Bobb to cancel the show. The ACLU fired off a missive to the city threatening to sue on behalf of ticket holders if this course of action was followed. They also got in touch with the band's attorneys, who endorsed the suit and also decided to serve as plaintiffs alongside ticket holders. While the lawyers were preparing the suit, the ACLU speculates, the city attorney made the council aware that Bobb's decision wouldn't hold up in court.

Yet a representative from the Richmond city clerk's office told the on-line news service *Allstar* that Bobb had been the recipient of "numerous complaints, by phone and mail, from the residents of Richmond and the surrounding jurisdictions and [we] are still getting them." Eventually the city council released a public statement addressing the concerns of distressed citizens as well as those of the city administration, but concluded that "despite these concerns, based upon the advice of the City Attorney, the city of Richmond will allow the concert to go forward as planned." The band's representatives had assured the good people of Richmond that they would abide by all applicable laws, recognizing that "any violation of law by any party during the performance will be prosecuted."

The domino effect was in full swing now. The "Dead to the World" tour was set to culminate in America with a two-week stint on the road with Pantera, a reunited Black Sabbath, and other notorious heavy metal hard-hitters as part of Ozzy Osbourne's annual OzzFest. The ten dates were scheduled to barrel out of the starting gate on June 15th Giants Stadium in East Rutherford, New Jersey. But the New Jersey Sports and Exposition Authority decided the bill wasn't entirely to their liking, and announced that unless Manson were pulled off the bill, the concert wouldn't go on at all. "Giants Stadium officials cited security concerns, as well as the nature of

Manson's act, as the reason they'd failed to sign the contract with OzzFest for the scheduled show so long as Manson remained on the bill," *Amusement Business* reported. Citing First Amendment violations, Osbourne, Manson, and Delsener-Slater (the promoters for the OzzFest) filed an injunction against the NJSEA.

On April 18, Nasty Little Man, the publicists for OzzFest, released a statement with Ozzy Osbourne's responses to the threat that the show would be canceled if Marilyn Manson weren't pulled off the bill. "I will not be putting any limits on any of the OzzFests," he claimed, invoking the First Amendment and issues of civil liberty and freedom. "These shows are all about having a good time; I don't believe that anyone, regardless of age, should be prohibited by law from enjoying themselves at a rock show.

"But situations like this are cyclical," he continued. "They tried to stop Elvis in the '50s, The Beatles in the '60s, [the Stanley Kubrick film] *A Clockwork Orange* in the '70s and Ozzy Osbourne in the '80s. There are always people who want to impose their standards on you by any means necessary. Blackmail is a stain on free society, and I will not give in to it on any level."

Three weeks later, on May 7, the conflict was resolved in a New Jersey federal district court. Judge Alfred Wolin ruled that there was no legal reason why Manson shouldn't be allowed to perform, particularly since ten other heavy metal bands on the bill hadn't raised an eyebrow from the Giants Stadium officials. Wolin also felt that the NJSEA had failed to "show cause" as to why Manson should be banned from the venue. As Jeff Gold observed for the Associated Press: "The band has done nothing wrong and no laws have been broken."

As the old saying goes, there's no rest for the wicked. Unfortunately, the next obstacle in Manson's path was hardly a laughing matter. The May 9 show at D.C. Armory in Washington, D.C., turned out to be the subject of media attention for an altogether different, and tragic reason. A member of the lighting crew, thirty-year-old Sean McGann (not Sean Beavan, as many rumors erroneously purported), died when he fell from a catwalk suspended ninety feet from the floor of the D.C. Armory complex. Evidence suggested that McGann and some friends had been drinking and rappelling down a wall in the facility when the accident occurred. Although the authorities later decided that no foul play was involved, members of the Manson entourage were questioned, and the show was delayed.

In the midst of all the legal imbroglios and on- and offstage mishaps, the *New Musical Express* managed (as only the UK music press can) to drum up a humorous twist on all the brouhaha surrounding Marilyn Manson. In a short news blurb, they disclosed that the father of Welsh trio 60 Ft. Dolls' drummer Carl Bevan wanted the group's gig scheduled for May 19 to be called off. Pastor Ray Bevan of King's Church in Newport announced that he intended to picket at the venue if the gig went ahead. The good reverend, who'd been a member of sixties pop band Robbie Ray & the Jaguars (who once cut a musical rendition of the Lord's Prayer), claimed, "I really don't think this concert should go ahead at all. It sounds very dangerous and the promoters and those who have booked the concert have a responsibility not to let this go ahead." The *NME* went on to quote a spokesperson for the Dolls: "We support the Pastor Ray Bevan and think Marilyn Manson should get banned because they're crap." The show went ahead as scheduled.

FOURTEEN

AFTER A MONTH OF European dates, the band returned to America to hook up with Ozzy Osbourne's OzzFest. In an amusing cover story planned months ahead, *Guitar World* magazine had brought these two notorious figures together. "Back when I was 15 years old, I never would've thought that one day I'd be playing a tour with Ozzy Osbourne. It's great being a part of something that had an impact on you when you were growing up," Manson gushed. Osbourne was equally complimentary, and as the conversation between the two unfurled, they turned out to have much in common, including extensive battles with agents of the Christian church, and even similar tales of woe concerning not receiving proper security or medical assistance in conservative corners of Texas.

Unfortunately, Black Sabbath fans seemed to have trouble bridging the cultural gap, no matter how narrow, that did exist between the two artists. Many reviews of the OzzFest shows centered around the fact that Marilyn Manson seemed out of their element, constricted to a tight forty-minute opening slot, and facing an audience that—though it certainly contained pockets of Spooks—consisted largely of hard-core mosh pit devotees (out to catch Pantera and their like) and old-school Sabbath/Osbourne fans. In this environment, the band didn't seem nearly as threatening. "While Manson was nearly banned from the show, Pantera, whose last album flirted more overtly with fascism, and whose guitarist, Dimebag Darrell, plays a Confederate flag–adorned ax, raised no objections," critic Eric Weisbard acutely observed in an especially biting *SPIN* review.

Once again, local authorities at several dates of the OzzFest mounted legal challenges to attempt to prevent the band from playing, and protestors came out in force at shows like the Apple River Ampitheatre one in Sommerset, Wisconsin. The band took their lumps and put on the best show they could. But their patience was wearing thin. "It got annoying when people were trying to cancel our shows because they didn't really understand what the band was about," Manson told Murray Engleheart for *Allstar*. These were people who hadn't seen the popular videos for "The Beautiful People" or "Tourniquet" on MTV, or heard the songs on the radio. No, their background information on Marilyn Manson was coming from resources like the mysterious "affidavits" in cyberspace.

Finally, in the June 26 issue of *Rolling Stone*, in the story "Stage Fright," Manson fought back. The singer, who told the magazine he planned to sue parties who posted misinformation concerning the band on-line, decided to dispel the bigger lies himself. Why would he throw drugs into the audience, he laughed, when he could be backstage doing them himself? As for charges of animal abuse, he pointed out that he was a pet owner (he'd spoken lovingly of his canine charge, Lydia, back in the pages of *huH*: "It's a girl dog, but I wanted a boy dog so I sometimes call her Walter. I've trained her to have a split personality."). Accusations of devil worship were met with lucid answers as to the nature of the Church of Satan, and his involvement, saying he considered himself as much a member of Anton LaVey's congregation as that of St. Paul's Episcopal back in Canton (where he'd been baptized) or Blockbuster Video. Onstage rapes incited by the band? "Now how could somebody actually believe that I could be involved in something like that and I wouldn't be in prison?" he responded.

But Manson was getting tired of helping advertise the efforts of his adversaries. Christianity had taken up quite a bit of his time and attention, since a very early age. The very steps he'd taken away from it had only steeped him further in the aspects of it he most disdained. Yet even after all he'd endured, Manson still did a passable job of turning the other cheek, reminding *Allstar* subscribers that he didn't disdain the tenets of Christianity, just how some people inverted them to suit an agenda. "As far as the religious groups go, I think I'm very open-minded," he said. "I don't protest Sunday schools or try to burn down churches. I'm always trying to learn different things from different people, and I think if someone feels secure in their beliefs, they shouldn't be afraid to let somebody else speak their mind as well."

Ultimately, despite the clamor around the band, Manson wasn't too enthusiastic with how the festival shows had gone. The older demographic had clearly disfavored Marilyn Manson, who he also admitted weren't used to opening slots anymore. "There were a lot of people there that hadn't heard us before. It was interesting to be hated and to confuse people once again, because we're used to playing in front of our fans." Hostility could provoke them to putting on a better show ("Anger is an energy," as Johnny Lydon once sang), although it's helpful to recall Paula O'Keefe's observations that Manson fares far less well with indifferent audiences. But if they were truly rotten, all the better. "I got hit with a bottle of piss," he concluded in *Allstar,* "but that wasn't anything that really bothered me."

EVEN AS THE SEEMINGLY endless touring in support of *Antichrist Superstar* wound down (with much of July off, followed by a handful of Canadian dates, some of which didn't occur, resulting in threats of more lawsuits), Manson managed to keep busy throughout the summer, making New York City his base of operations. On several occasions he was spotted entertaining at an S and M theme restaurant in Manhattan named La Nouvelle Justine (named for a novel by the Marquis de Sade). The band and their friends carried on in the boîte's medieval-dungeon splendor, while savoring cocktails with tantalizing names like the Coprophiliac (no doubt a favorite of Ginger's, if he remembered Albert Fish's repulsive eating habits) and the

Infantilist, and delighted in tormenting fellow patrons. On one no-table evening, a petulant businessman in professional attire disap-peared into the men's room, and returned to offer himself up to the band . . . dressed as a schoolgirl, complete with plaits.

At the end of July, Manson announced yet another bizarre install-ment in the evolution of the Marilyn Manson phenomenon. HarperCollins had purchased the rights to publish his memoirs. "I'm writing an autobiography that'll be out before the end of the year," he revealed to the on-line magazine *Allstar*. "I'm just telling a few stories I think people will be interested in hearing," he added. His tentative title? *The World Spreads Its Legs for Another Star*. Rumor has it he was so excited about the project, he rushed out and bought a Dictaphone and several thesauri, then contacted a prominent *New York Times* music critic to lend a discreet hand to the labor.

Maybe the heat got to him, but Manson felt the need to strip off a few layers on one especially memorable occasion. Fans that wanted to see even more of their idol were soon rushing out to snag hard-to-find copies of the August issue of the pornographic page-turner *Hustler*. A few weeks earlier, the music industry trade magazine *Hits* had leaked that the singer would indulge in full-frontal nudity for the layout. This marked a step in a raunchier direction compared to his previous foray into the porn world. In the April 1996 issue of *Rave*, Manson had cavorted with hardcore actress Marylin Star (who wore a strap-on dildo of her own for many of the pictures), but hadn't actually revealed the Warner family jewels. But the *Hustler* captioning proved especially harsh. A shot of Manson getting a blow job read: "Some people don't like Marilyn's music; this shot proves it's actually his fans who suck." Another one, which depicted him chomping down on a woman's derriere, declared, "Marilyn Manson, biting as hard as his warmed over Alice Cooper schtick."

The Cooper connection had been brought up countless times in the past. But not long after the *Hustler* publication, the elder statesman of shock rock brought up the topic himself in an interview with writer Murray Engleheart. "A guy with a girl's name and makeup and [who] does theatrics. I wonder where I've heard that before? It's just shocking," he joked. Cooper seemed to consider Manson's success as a form of homage, even though in the past the younger performer had derided his onetime hero for toning down his act, returning to the Christian faith, and becoming a vocal proponent of the sport of golf. But the former Vince Furnier didn't seem to have an especially firm handle on the MM aesthetic anyway. "The only thing that's probably very, very much different from our approaches to music is the fact they're industrial and we're pretty hard rock, and at the same time they kind of dabble in this occult thing where we're much more just fantasy theatrics."

New musical contributions from the band cropped up in several odd places, too, including the sound track to *Spawn,* a motion picture based on the popular comic by Todd MacFarlane. Executive producer Happy Walters had previously wed hip-hop and alternative bands to great effect on the album for *Judgement Night.* Now he sought to do the same by pairing an even wider assortment of rock contributors with some of the biggest luminaries in electronic dance music. Marilyn Manson collaborated with UK trip-hop trio Sneaker Pimps on a new Manson/Ramirez composition, "The Long Hard Road Out of Hell" (yet another reference to Milton's epic poem *Paradise Lost*). "It was really so much fun," the Pimps songbird Kelli Dayton told *Alternative Press.* "The other guys [in Sneaker Pimps] aren't really into dark-sounding things." Dayton, however, voiced her fondness for Sisters of Mercy and the Cramps. "But the whole point to the Sneaker Pimps is that we are not limited to one thing."

That said, they did enter the collaboration with a bit of trepidation. "We were kind of nervous about the Marilyn Manson thing," multi-instrumentalist/producer Liam Howe revealed. In the end, everyone involved seemed to enjoy him- or herself. "It all made sense, kind of like Run-DMC and Aerosmith's 'Walk This Way.' At first it was weird, like kissing someone that wasn't your sort." The Pimps complained that the version of the track that reached the final CD wasn't the one they'd approved, but that didn't stop the Epic label from releasing "The Long Hard Road . . ." as the album's second single.

Meanwhile, Manson and Twiggy, with an assist from Sean Beavan, added a little juice to the single "Transylvanian Concubine," by the Traveling Ladies Cello Society known as Rasputina. The trio of string players had toured with Marilyn Manson earlier in the year, providing a musical interlude in between the thundering sets of Helmet and the headliners. Manson had been so taken with audiences' reactions to the eerie antics of the threesome (who perform in vintage corsets) that he even asked them to provide ethereal backing vocals. Manson's distinctive derivation of the band's music was featured in two versions on the *Transylvanian Regurgitations* EP, "The Manson Mix" and the longer "Yes Sir, Mr. Sir Mix." "The remix we did while we were on the road with them," Manson revealed, "and I think it scared them because the song was a 3/4 sort of waltz number, and we replaced it with a 4/4 Ice Cube drum beat, [with] death metal guitars on it."

Fans who had been perched before the VCR, waiting with bated breath to see Manson's appearance on Bill Maher's talk show *Politically Incorrect* on July 30 ended up having to wait an additional two weeks when the episode was bumped. "It had nothing to do with censorship and everything about ratings," a spokesperson for the show claimed. The Manson slot had been bumped until ratings were better; the notion that the shock rocker would probably generate plenty seemed to miss them.

When the episode finally aired on Wednesday, August 13, Manson was polite and levelheaded, and looked smashing in a black suit and skinny tie, his eyes framed with yellowish green makeup. Given the lineup of participants, the broadcast should've have been historic television, as the singer was joined by actress Florence Henderson of *Brady Bunch* fame, and author/media personality/Watergate criminal G. Gordon Liddy. Unfortunately, the fourth invitee, "abstinence advocate" and rap artist Lakita Garth, dominated the discussion, trying to rankle Manson and failing miserably, even as she managed to annoy everyone else on the stage. Among the rare bright moments, Liddy chided Manson for taking Nietzsche out of context, and the shameless Henderson mugged and announced that she and Manson were "going to the prom together." Manson did manage to fire off one especially memorable line when pressed on his views about the Bible. "People can see Christ as a lot like me," he quipped. "I have long hair. I have fans, he had twelve disciples, that could be his posse."

And throughout the summer months, Manson was a frequent face at rock shows, from the Tibetan Freedom Concert on Randall's Island in New York, to a quiet supper club show by Seattle scenesters Brad. But for all his notoriety, he still seemed the odd man out in some crowds, and suffered from occasional bouts of the cheese stands alone. After a gig by Radiohead on August 26, Manson and friends followed the band to a party at the Spy Bar. The strangeness started even before the guests of honor arrived, when designer Calvin Klein showed up and flashed a peek of his famous undergarments to Manson, noting that "the fit's great." Whether he was trying to pitch Manson on the product's allure, or seduce him into some sort of advertising deal is uncertain. Either way, Klein would undoubtedly have been delighted to learn that the singer already favors his popular boxer briefs.

However, when Radiohead's front man Thom Yorke materialized, he opted to schmooze with the members of the Scottish band Teenage Fanclub instead. Manson urged Yorke to sit down with his entourage, saying that there was plenty of room on the club's expansive sofas. But Yorke seemed a little shaken by the invite, and just waved graciously, exchanged hellos, and held court with Fanclub at the bar.

BY SEPTEMBER 4, MARILYN Manson seemed to have attained all they'd initially dreamed of, and perhaps a bit more. They'd just returned from a triumphant show with Metallica at England's Reading Festival. In a few hours, they'd take the stage at the MTV Video Music Awards (Manson wisely declined to comment on his feelings concerning sharing the stage with the Spice Girls), and devastate the audience by closing the ceremonies with a rendition of "The Beautiful People" that highlighted another one of Manson's infamous revealing outfits. And in a few days, they'd enter the studio to begin work on the follow-up to *Antichrist Superstar*.

And although the news wouldn't be made public for several weeks, two days earlier the former Daisy Berkowitz had filed a suit in Broward County Circuit Court, Florida, under his birth name Scott Putesky. Naming Brian "Marilyn Manson" Warner, Marilyn Manson (the band), and their Los Angeles attorney, David Codikow, as defendants, the artist now known as Scott Mitchell sought fifteen million dollars in compensatory damages for "breach of contract, breach of fiduciary duty, professional legal malpractice and fraudulent inducement to conversion." The suit claimed that not only had Scott never received proper recognition for his role in the band's conception, but that after signing to Nothing Records, Codikow had encouraged the group to draw up a partnership agreement that unfairly granted Warner exclusive control of the moniker *Marilyn Manson*.

But for now, the task at hand was delivering the keynote address at the prestigious CMJ Music Marathon. The same industry figures and budding music biz types that three years ago had dismissed Marilyn Manson as Trent Reznor's puppet, a mere vanity project for a man playing label boss, had watched Manson's power and popularity swell over the course of the past thirty-six months. Now they'd come to hear the great man speak. As usual, Manson handled the affair with his typical mix of humility, insight, and caustic humor.

"I'm not good at speeches," he began. "I guess a year ago we came here to do a Night of Nothing Showcase, which ended in a disaster of my drummer going in the hospital, and since then, the things that have happened weren't any surprise to me. I thought making the album was going to be transformational, but recording it was even more. And it's only through self-contempt and inward dying that you can really become yourself. And that's what I tried to do.

"And with anything that I've ever done, with songs or performance, has always been to make people think. So I feel that that's part of rock and roll that's in danger of extinction. I think it's pointless for me to get up here and talk about the defects and the faults of mankind today because when you get right down to it, we're all just a bunch of monkeys, and whenever we try and be anything more than that is when we hurt each other."

With those words, he opened the floor to questions, and fielded a reasonably worthwhile round of inquiries. One response in particular seemed especially promising. Considering the important role controversy had played in spreading Marilyn Manson's messages, one fan queried, how did Manson expect to continue developing when the uproar died down? Would his career fizzle and be finished?

"It could be if I was that naïve," he admitted. "But like I said, this is just the beginning for me, and I think to prove Marilyn Manson as a musical force and for people to really sit down and listen to an album like *Antichrist Superstar* and the one we're about to record, controversy is just something extra. I don't think that's what I'm about. I will prove that to everyone."